About the author

Bryony Hill is married to football legend Jimmy Hill. She lived in France and London before settling in rural Sussex. Bryony wrote and illustrated *A Compost Kind of Girl*, about the development of her garden, and has published a cookbook, *Angel in an Apron*, *Penalty Chick*, a novel about being a footballer's wife, and *How I Long to be With You - War Letters Home*, a collection of family letters and documents reflecting the realities of life during the Second World War.

By the same author and published by Book Guild

Penalty Chick (2003)
A Compost Kind of Girl (2007)
Angel in an Apron (2010)
How I Long to be With You – War Letters Home (2014)

MY GENTLEMAN JIM

Bryony Hill

Book Guild Publishing

First published in Great Britain in 2015 by
The Book Guild Ltd
9 Priory Business Park
Wistow Road
Kibworth
Leics LE8 0RX
Email: info@bookguild.co.uk
Freephone: 0800 999 2982
Web: www.bookguild.co.uk
Twitter: @bookguild

Typesetting in Garamond by
YHT Ltd, London

Printed and bound in Great Britain by
CPI Group (UK) Ltd, Croydon, CR0 4YY

A catalogue record for this book is available from
The British Library.

ISBN 978 1 910508 93 0

To Jimmy, the yang to my yin.

Jimmy Hill was a visionary. His flair and energy ended soccer's maximum wage slavery, changed the face of soccer on TV, turned Coventry City, a dying football club, into an establishment that held its own in the top flight for 34 years and revitalised the league system with three points for a win; a force of football nature and a true gent besides.

—Baron Grade of Yarmouth CBE

As a fellow supporter of SPARKS since its earliest days Jimmy has been instrumental in maintaining the link between the sporting community and medical research, benefiting the lives of children throughout the world. As well as being a legend of football and a larger-than-life personality, Jimmy has always been a passionate champion of good causes.

—Her Royal Highness Princess Michael of Kent

Contents

CONTENTS

I was a great footballer you know. In 1956, I was up for Footballer of the Year and I said to the missus, 'You could be sleeping with the Footballer of the Year tonight.' We got to the ceremony and the announcer said: 'In third place, Tom Finney, in second place, Wandering Walter, in first place, Stanley Matthews.' My missus said, 'Is Stanley Matthews coming here or do I need to go to him?'
—Wandering Walter (1929-2013)

Foreword

For football people of my generation, Jimmy Hill is an iconic figure. He dominated our TV screens, and his forthright opinions and desire to implement change made a difference to our lives. Perhaps the most influential change Jimmy brought about in his capacity as Chairman of the Professional Footballers' Association was the abolition of the maximum wage in 1961, thus enabling players to take their rightful share of the money being generated by the game. His championing of all-seater football stadia and the idea of three points for a win were two further important initiatives which we take for granted today.

When Jimmy moved over to television, first with ITV and then on to the BBC to present *Match of the Day*, we witnessed the start of football punditry and analysis, which not only popularised the sport even more but also acted as a tool for insight, education and entertainment, helping fans to understand the game further.

My first encounter with Jimmy was from the terraces at Fulham FC during his playing days. Later I was to do several TV interviews with him before finally enjoying the pleasure of his company when he returned to Fulham, the club he loved, during my time as manager there. Intelligence, courtesy, vision and a down-to-earth approach to life are not always qualities which we associate with football leaders. They are, though, qualities for which we should strive, and Jimmy Hill therefore is someone whom we look up to and respect and thank for his unparalleled contribution to the beautiful game.

Congratulations to Bryony for writing this book and, for giving us an even greater insight into the man whose place on a football roll of honour was assured long ago.

Roy Hodgson, England National Football Team Manager

Acknowledgements

Under normal circumstances this is where I would list all those dear people who have helped me get this story off the ground, but in this instance – and I hope I shall be forgiven – I will leave it to our friend Mark Pearman to speak on behalf of the man himself, without whom this venture would not have been possible. Mark also volunteered to check my manuscript for any mistakes concerning some of the more challenging football fences, thus preventing me from pecking on landing.

I wish to give a special mention to the late Alan Williams, a Fulham fan through and through, whose widow Beryl permitted me to use her husband's portrait of Jimmy for the front cover. Also to Paul Keevil who took the perfect picture of Jimmy and Charlie. Paul came to our house when Charlie was a six-month-old puppy to take photographs for a forthcoming article in *Dogs Today* magazine. Instead of wrapping things up quickly, he stayed the entire day and said afterwards that it was one of the most enjoyable commissions he had ever experienced. Last but not least my everlasting gratitude goes to Carol Biss and my friend and agent Laura Longrigg.

Here is the touching tribute by Mark, who was Jimmy's editor at Sky on *The Last Word*:

As a young boy growing up in the Seventies, like many others, my passion was football. Fuelled by its presence on TV and the relative success of Ipswich Town (my local club), I lived and breathed the game and the heroes who would entertain me most Saturday nights. Football was for my generation what the Internet or iPhone is to today's. Our street was full of those who thought they could become professionals, and, when colour television arrived, it intensified this dream.

Jimmy was a 'must watch', from his sharp, authoritative delivery to his very stylish wardrobe, his insight of the game, his opinions and his conclusions were a massive part of my growing up; he was one of the family. His celebrity was often bigger than that of the stars on show, and certainly bigger than some of the games that were broadcast, but he was never pompous or too self-important to relate to the common people ... After all, he was one underneath.

My father was told at my school parents' evening that unless I forgot about being a professional footballer, I would be a failure in life. Another teacher remarked that I would never have a career in the sport, so what was the point in wasting my time playing and thinking about it? In 1983 I left for London aged 17 and stumbled across a part-time job at the BBC. Six years later, as an assistant producer on *Match of the Day*, I was on a plane to Newcastle for their FA Cup 5th round match against Manchester United. Des [Lynam] was fronting and Jimmy was the pundit. On the flight home I sat next to Jim. Aware of his celebrity, I tried to keep a respectful silence, so as not to embarrass myself nor disturb him. However, before the engines rolled, it was he who befriended me for that journey, during which he demonstrated his warmth, and was giving in conversation and generous with his advice.

Before we landed, he discovered he had mislaid his car keys, but he stayed carefree and jovial despite knowing he would have to phone home to get someone to come and pick him up when he got back to Heathrow. To him, such an inconvenience was one of those things. I pinched myself that evening. It was not so much that I was awestruck by his presence, it was more that, unlike some whom I had met in the industry, he presented himself as a very sociable and decent man. To work with him so closely some years later at Sky Sports was a pleasure, and our friendship evolved. We attended many social events together and I enjoyed watching Jimmy holding court. He had enormous class and could relate to and converse with anyone, from king to serf.

There is little doubt that he loved the adulation and, naturally, anyone that successful and so much in demand would have an ego. There's nothing wrong in that. But outside the TV industry and at his home in Sussex he remained someone I admired and looked up to. He waxed lyrical about the life in the country, as it was such a contrast to his working life's demands. He was always so proud of Bryony; how she found great pleasure in the simple things in life and the projects she threw herself into. He was very lucky to find her, although I'm not that blinkered to think it could have been very tough living with the old boy!

I will never forget the friendship and generosity both Jim and Bryony bestowed on my family.

This book is a loveling tribute to their life together, and I would like to thank Bryony for putting the same devotion into its creation as she has into caring for Jim. He would be so proud.

Prologue: The Swinging Sixties

Name Drops Keep Falling On My Head

My first brush with celebrity occurred on 31 August 1965, when I was nine months older than Adrian Mole. My friend Deborah and I had taken the train to London with the sole aim of trawling Carnaby Street in the West End, the best place to see pop stars we had gleaned from such publications as *Jackie* '(for go-ahead teens)', *16 Magazine* and *Fave!* I remember exactly what clothes I was wearing as if it were yesterday: navy blue T-bar kitten heels from Dolcis, white skinny rib top and lace stockings, a pale blue pencil skirt (with a Dior pleat) I'd made at school and my mother's boxy mustard-coloured Jaeger mohair car coat.

Debbie, nine months my senior, was far more stylish in her purple mini-skirt, black polo neck sweater and calf-length kinky boots, her hair smoothed into flick-ups catching the eye of every male we passed.

We hadn't been there for more than five minutes when she tugged my sleeve and, not believing our luck, we stared open-mouthed at a lanky, long-haired man stepping from a taxi. 'It's Keith Relf of the Yardbirds!' she squealed.

We marched into *His Clothes*, the trendy men's outfitters owned by John Stephen, the self-proclaimed 'King of Carnaby Street' and, over-excited by our early success, I spent far more than I could afford on a Shetland pullover for my older brother Paul.

This is the entry from my diary for that year, that sums up how it felt to be a teenager in 1965:

In the shop were Mick Jagger and Keith Richards [both then aged 21], trying on jackets. I noticed them and nearly fell over

1

backwards. Mick kept on looking at us, as we were the only girls there, and smiling. We went out, waited, and walked on, stopping at another shop. They followed us and must have been walking damn fast, as they stopped and stood right behind us, leaning over and talking to each other. I saw Keith's reflection and caught his eye and we burst into laughter. Mick was about two inches away from Debbie's face and breathed down her neck; she said, 'Excuse us', and made them move so we could walk away. We hid in a phone box and saw Mick and Keith giving some silly girls their autographs but we wouldn't ask for them as it's against our principals [*sic*]!

That December Debbie returned to Carnaby Street, and while she was queuing in a crowded shop to pay for a book (my Christmas present), it was whipped from her hand by none other than Mick, who insisted he wouldn't give it back unless she went and had a coffee with him. Needless to say, she agreed, and she told me later that when the waitress carried their cups to their table she was shaking so much most of it slopped into the saucers.

We must have made quite an impression on Mick back in the summer because he remembered having seen both of us and, unbelievably, our outfits. 'I fancied you,' he confirmed to Debbie, 'and Keith fancied your mate.' There but for the grace of God ...

Debbie wrote a note to me accompanying her gift: 'Mick invited me to David Bailey's party, which is tonight, but I'm not going. Daren't tell M & D [Mum and Dad] that I met Mick again. Hope you like the enclosed. I begged him to write in it and I said you were v. ill.'

That I was at death's door was an absolute fib of course - I was as fit as a flea - but Debbie thought it wouldn't hurt to prey on his sympathy. Inside the cover, he had written in pencil (misspelling my name): 'To Byony [*sic*] with love from Mick as well'. He asked which school Debbie went to, but all she would divulge was that it was in Kent. It didn't take a degree in rocket science to work out that she might be a pupil at Benenden, and at the beginning of the autumn term a letter (the first of many) arrived at the school addressed simply to 'Deborah'. 'I'm afraid,' she wrote to me, 'I've got some rather disappointing news for you (this is purely to make you jealous!) I got a postcard from Mick in Cairo on his way to Australia for a two-week tour.'

Nearly half a century on from that adolescent celebrity-fuelled thrill, I have had to watch helplessly as Jimmy buckles under the extruding tentacles of Alzheimer's disease. In finding the inspiration to write our love story, I have been able once again to live with the man, comforted by the mountain of memories we thought would keep us warm in our old age. Because of his ill health he is no longer able to answer my questions or provide me with anecdotes and, my own recall not as total as I would wish, I have had to dig out dusty press cuttings, rummage through boxes of letters, listen to taped interviews and study his own, precious scribblings. I pray you can still hear his oh-so-familiar voice – and sense of humour.

I unearthed so much 'stuff' I was overwhelmed with the daunting task of sorting the wheat from the chaff. Gritting my teeth, I battled on – and I'm glad I did, because it led to an emotional catharsis: a monumental mishmash of acute sadness and joy, but one which helped me get through some very dark days. When the spectre of the Black Dog snapped at my ankles once too often I gained strength in one of Jimmy's favourite homilies, which was: 'In order to know where you are going you have to learn to appreciate and understand where you have been.'

Our friendship and love span nigh on four decades (by Jimmy's playful reckoning, the equivalent of two life sentences), and nothing, not even this baffling illness, can rob us of the cherished moments we shared.

For many years we took part in an annual charity tournament organised by brewer Tony Ruddle at Stoke Rochford Golf Club near Grantham in Lincolnshire to raise funds for the Mental Health Foundation. After we were back off the course, with a whistle wetter at the 19th followed by lunch, Princess Diana's sister Lady Sarah McCorquodale, who lived nearby, dropped in to present the prizes. It was a relaxed affair, and Sarah turned up on another afternoon in shorts and flip-flops, accompanied by her children. Tony's relations and friends ran the competition; one of them was John Hawkes-worth, the film and television producer (and very competent watercolour artist).

John is probably best remembered for his involvement with ITV's perennially popular series *Upstairs, Downstairs*. He also produced, in 1959, the crime drama film *Tiger Bay* starring the legendary Sir John Mills. The part of the young child (witness to a murder) was originally written for a boy, but John was not happy with any of those whom he auditioned. Then, in a burst of inspiration, he cast Sir John's young daughter Hayley in the role, which launched her acting career and for which she won a BAFTA award as Most Promising Newcomer.

It was always a treat to catch up with the Hawkesworths, and I contacted John when I first had the urge to write. A very busy man, he took the time to respond with a long, two-page letter on foolscap paper, giving me invaluable advice that I have tried ever since to follow.

One year when I was waiting with my team on the first tee for John to give us the go-ahead he said that, by living longer, we faced an ever-increasing challenge; he gave the shattering statistics that, on average, one in four people needs some sort of help during their lifetime. Unfortunately, ageing and mental health are not considered 'fashionable' or even, God forbid, 'sexy', and therefore it is tough getting people to dip into their pockets to fund research. Maybe it's high time we adjusted our attitude and loosened our purse strings.

My Gentleman Jim is a wonderfully indulgent, loving celebration of our life together. When I started to make a list of Jimmy's achievements, I was fully aware of the danger of pitching head first into a cavernous sycophantic trap. Then I remembered another of his favourite adages: 'the opposite of doing nothing is to do something'.

Unlike me, with my roots firmly embedded in a typical middle-class upbringing, Jimmy started out in life from humbler beginnings. The only thing we shared was that we were both born in the front room of our family homes, me in an oak-beamed, timber-framed cottage in Sussex, and Jimmy in a modest mid-terrace Victorian villa in Balham, a million years from the trendy London suburb it has since become.

Although a bright pupil, he left school after taking Matric, choosing to start earning a living in order to help his parents rather than continue his education at university. One of his first jobs was as a baker's boy alongside his father, delivering bread in South London and, with the knowledge he garnered, he prided himself on being able to recognise the attributes of a well-made loaf.

Eventually he broke loose from the paternal apron strings to become a sales rep for a light-bulb manufacturer, followed by a period as a chimney sweep for the Immaculate Chimney Sweeping Company. The business, owned by Ossie Noble, was in addition to Ossie's other profession, that of music hall artist. In need of a side-kick in his act, he asked Jimmy to join him occasionally on stage.

This eclectic professional career continued with number crunching (something at which he excelled) at the Stock Exchange, then the summons of National Service, followed by professional footballer, journalist, broadcaster, charity champion, Pipe Man of the Year in 1971 and 1972 (awarded by the Briar Pipe and Trade Association) and all-round good sport.

Derek Ufton (centre half for Charlton FC, wicket-keeper for Kent) has perhaps known my husband longer than anyone else. He told me:

I first met Jimmy in October 1946 on a very wet day on a muddy football field in a village in Gloucestershire. It was an away match and we were playing for the Royal Army Service Corps unit based at Cirencester. We were both aged eighteen and had served our initial six weeks' basic training before being posted there to await a WOSB [War Office Selection Board], as potential officers. We had volunteered for the soccer team and found ourselves representing our new base in the second division of the local football league. We won the match and were trying to wash the mud off ourselves with water – very cold – from the only, very small, bucket provided. We started chatting, got on the lorry, which took us back to the base and, on disembarking, agreed to meet that evening (it was a Saturday) at the camp's gymnasium where a dance was being held.

Arriving together, we entered the vast hall. We were about the first to arrive, and those present were in uniform, mostly

Army, some RAF, and more girls than fellers. What we both noticed immediately was the quality of the music. There was a large stage at one end and it was filled by a 'big band', so popular in those days. We listened for half an hour to them play when Jimmy said, 'This is ridiculous. The music is superb and it's wasted. I'm going to have a word with that chap on the sax; he seems to be the leader.'

At the next break Jim jumped onto the platform, had a quick word with the saxophone player, grabbed the mike and announced, 'The next dance is a waltz to the music of the RAF South Cerney Band, led by Johnny Dankworth.' Jimmy continued to act as MC for the rest of the evening and agreed to be in attendance again the following Wednesday. I don't know whether it was Johnny Dankworth's music or Jimmy's MC-ing, but that gym was full to the seams and everybody danced.

A couple of weeks later the trumpeter fell ill and Jimmy mentioned he had played the cornet in the Boys' Brigade. He filled in and even attempted 'Golden Earrings' as a solo. I realised I'd met an extraordinary talent, two in fact, as Johnny Dankworth became a household name.

We continued to have success on the field but failed the WOSB in March. We were disappointed but assumed it was because they didn't need officers now that the war was over. We were due to be posted and fortunately more or less got the postings we wanted near to London and our homes. [Jimmy had bought an iron to keep his kit in tiptop shape and, by pressing the other squaddies' uniforms for a fee, he earned enough money to pay for the trip home to Balham each weekend, only missing out once for the entire duration of his National Service.]

Jimmy went to Blackdown and I went to Buller Barracks nearby in Aldershot and played for the RASC cricket team. At the end of the season one of the officers asked me if I also played soccer. I said, 'Yes,' and two days later I was despatched to No. 3 Training Battalion, Farnborough, in Hampshire – home of the RASC soccer team, which harboured ambitions of winning the Army Cup.

The season began and we had quite a good team. The officers

in charge called a meeting and declared we needed a big, strong inside forward who would score goals. Did anyone have any ideas? Nobody said a word until I said, 'There was a chap I played with at Cirencester called Jimmy Hill who scored a lot of goals.' Three days later I looked out of my office window and there was Jimmy, walking down the road, rifle over one shoulder, kit bag over the other. I rushed out to meet him, he glared at me and said, 'You wait till I get the idiot who has done this! I had everything going for me at Blackdown. I've just been made a corporal running the Pay Office; I've got a super billet and the best-looking girl in the area. I am really very fed up.' He didn't find out I was the one who had ruined his prospects until 50 years later when I told the story to Michael Aspel on *This is Your Life*.

When the idea for *My Gentleman Jim* was in embryonic form I mentioned it to Mark (Pearman), who said that, when he reads a book, he wants to learn something he didn't already know. Another, whom I press-ganged into wading through my first draft (and second – poor devil), flattered me by saying I had 'written a moving and most interesting story'.

When researching *How I Long To Be With You: War Letters Home* (Book Guild Publishing, November 2014), I called in to see Dame Vera Lynn at her home in the village of Ditchling at the foot of the South Downs not far from where we live.

Over tea and lemon drizzle cake, Vera, now nudging a century, recounted some of her experiences when on tour in Burma during the Second World War, showing me mementoes and photographs taken when entertaining 'our boys' in the Far East. During our conversation she asked after Jimmy, whom she had known for decades through her charity work or when we bumped into each other, usually in front of the fish counter at our local supermarket or at the bank. After a moment's contemplation she said, 'I wonder. Which is worse? Losing control of your body or your mind? We have no choice in the matter.'

Part One
The Seventies – Balls

1

The Elephant in the Room

Inside the Cottage: Fulham Football Club Official Programme, Saturday, 15 March 1952. Fulham v Arsenal:

For the second time this season we were concerned in an important exchange deal when we allowed Jimmy Bowie to go to Brentford in return for the signature of Jimmy Hill, Brentford's prominent right-half. We have reason to believe we have done good business. We have inside forwards to spare but are not so well blessed with first-class half-backs. Hill comes to us with a very big reputation and we are confident that we can put his ability to the best possible advantage. He was on Brentford's transfer list at his own request, and we are happy to have him. Hill very soon made his first appearance for us. He played right-half at Blackpool, Macaulay [Archibald, inside-forward/wing-half], going inside-right with the attack reading: Stevens [Arthur, outside-right], Campbell [Johnny, outside-left], Jeff Taylor [centre-forward] and Mitten [Charlie, outside-left]. The lads faded in the second half and allowed Blackpool to take the initiative. Stan Mortensen made Blackpool 3-2, one of his scoring shots scraping the post as it went in, and we scored two goals to get back into the picture. The first came from Jimmy Hill who went right through and scored with a great shot.

It has to be discussed. I can't avoid it.

'What?' you ask.

'Football,' I reply.

Forgive me, but I have never understood the dedication and obsession people share for what is arguably our national game. At

11

the risk of missing out on such joys, I prefer to snuggle up in front of a roaring fire to watch an old weepie on television rather than suffer 90 minutes of torture (both physical and mental) outside in all weathers. And here I am married to a man whose entire life and career have centred on the sport and who, each Saturday afternoon, checked the results: first Coventry City, then Fulham, followed by Charlton and Brentford – the four clubs with which he has been closely linked.

I must be one of the oldest WAGs in the business but, having not owned a hair dryer for more years than I care to remember, as far as I am concerned those three letters stand for 'Wash And Go'. On our first anniversary (it being paper), I presented Jimmy with a 1958 edition of the *Eagle* annual, number 7, that I had bought at a boot fair and in which, on page 20, there was an inspirational article entitled 'Put a Kick in Your Soccer by Jimmy Hill, Famous FA Coach of Fulham FC', the content of which holds good today.

'You do realise, Jimbo, that the cost of maintaining my hair comes to less than ten quid a year?'

'Ah,' he said thoughtfully, 'all these things, Miss B, were taken into careful consideration before I married you.'

You may wonder how in heaven's name I fell in love with England's Most Famous Footballer? Believe me, football had nothing to do with it.

Much of the population only know Jimmy as a television presenter/tub-thumper/chairman of a football club and are unaware that he actually kicked a ball about the park professionally. In fact he scored a very respectable total of 51 goals in his career – 10 for Brentford and 41 for Fulham – never once being presented with a yellow card or having his name taken, an honourable achievement he shared with Gary Lineker. He also liked to joke that, after retiring from the game, in the eyes of the public, the older he was, the better he became as a footballer. Therefore, for the less informed, I feel it my duty to fill in some of these gaps by putting historical flesh onto his octogenarian bones. And where better place to start than from his father's own hand?

William was fiercely proud of his son Jimmy, and this is clearly evident in what appears to be the beginnings of a biography written, in pencil, on pages torn from a 1954 diary:

Jimmy Hill was born in Pentney Road, Balham on 22 July 1928. He attended Cavendish Road School where he gained a scholarship and continued his education at Henry Thornton Secondary School, Clapham South Side. He matriculated at 16 years of age and although advised by his parents to stay on at school, he decided to leave. Had his parents pressed him to stay I feel sure he would have done so. Why didn't we press him? Well, Jimmy was an exceptional lad and seemed to be a few years older than he actually was. This was partly due to the fact that his stepsister and stepbrother were, respectively, 12 and 14 years his senior, and Jimmy is the type who learns from others, more than the average person. The last words from me regarding leaving school were: 'I don't want you to be a Prime Minister but I do want you to be able to earn enough to be able to live in normal comfort.' His reply was, 'I am confident I can do that.'

Jimmy learned his football at school, with the 88 Boys' Brigade and also when assisting the Dulwich Police Team before he was 16. Another club Jimmy played for was Sutton Home Guard and for the Balham League. He landed a job in the Stock Exchange until he was called up for National Service.

He joined the RASC and it was not long before it was discovered he could play football, also that he could run and he won the SW District 440 yards, but was unable to compete in the final owing to an injured foot. Folkestone FC in Kent spotted him and he guested for them as an inside-left, scoring many goals.

While he was in the Service Fulham got permission from his CO to play against Kettering Town for Fulham 'A' team. Before he returned to his unit the late Mr Peart, who was Fulham's manager, told him to come and see him when he left the Service. In the meantime however, he was asked if he would like to play for Reading.

When he eventually left the Service he went to see his old

boss at the Stock Exchange where they welcomed him back. I really think he would have been glad if they had said, 'We have no room for you,' as I feel sure he had football on his mind as a career. Then Ted Drake signed him on amateur terms for Reading FC. This was about three months before the end of the Season 1947–48 and [he] played regularly for Reading Reserves and began to be noticed. He asked Ted Drake to sign him as a professional but Reading had decided to look for local talent. 'But,' said Mr Drake, 'clubs have asked about you, among them Brentford, Fulham and Spurs.'

Jimmy was on Brentford's books as a professional and was playing for the first eleven during his first season. Naturally it was an ordeal and a section of the crowd did not help. Jimmy could have played a kick-and-kick game but when he learns any game, he first learns it theoretically and then puts it into practice and, by the way, don't challenge him at darts. Came the day at Brentford Jimmy dropped to half-back where he played a storming game and left the field with cheers and applause ringing in his ears. From then on he has never looked back, being selected at left-half for England 'B', also for FA Elevens and London FA v Germany. Bernard Joy [in the *Evening Standard*] predicted him among others as a star for the future.

He joined Fulham in March 1952 for whom he had played in seven different positions. He captained the team for a period until it was decided to let Johnny Haynes take over. Jimmy is also an FA coach and has been so for six years, during which time he coached Oxford University for two seasons. Jim Clarkson, the Middlesex Coaching Association secretary, told me he is one of their top coaches, with a great personality. Jimmy toured the West Indies with a Football Association team in 1955 and made many friends.

The following paragraphs appeared in the 'Cottage Crumbs' section of Fulham FC's *The Cottage Journal*:

The Summer holiday is over and we're down to the serious football business now, but no doubt you would like to know how some of the lads spent the break. Five of them – Bedford Jezzard, Johnny Haynes, Jimmy Hill, Bobby Robson and Robin Lawler – visited other parts of the world, to play football.

Bedford, Jimmy and Bobby were touring the West Indies with an FA XI. The trio said with one voice, 'It was a wonderful time. Magnificent. What beauty.' (They were referring to the islands!) 'What hospitality; what people.' Yes, we gathered, they enjoyed the trip.

Jimmy endorsed the team's enthusiasm in a postcard to his parents:

How would you like to spend a holiday here? The only trouble is that you become so thirsty that you need a fortune to spend on drinks. Rum is only 13/- a bottle in the shops but is 3/- a nip over the counter. We are all pretty suntanned but we have to keep in today for the match this afternoon. In the evenings we have had time to visit the local clubs for snooker, table tennis etc., which is a bit of a nuisance, as all the locals want to do is to talk football! The standard of football is not too good here. I only hope it stays that way.

This is his father's final paragraph:

When he was not playing he would broadcast the match on radio. He went again to the West Indies in the summer of 1956 but this time as a football coach and became very popular there. Again he found himself at the mike, broadcasting on his favourite game. In Jimmy's second season as a professional his father predicted that Jimmy would not only play for England but would captain England. But his chance, in my opinion, has been damned by his many activities, such as coaching, union activities, etc. But with the energy Jimmy possesses, physically and mentally, (ask Fulham supporters) he could still make the grade. Why did he not stick to playing football only? The real reason I am sure is a view to his future when his playing days are over.

2

Changes Afoot

In the back of Jimmy's diary for 2008 he compiled this list:

- Won scholarship to Grammar School
- Players promoted with Brentford and Fulham
- Played 7 positions for Fulham
- Highest living goal scorer (5) in League matches
- Removed maximum wage
- Manager – took Cov. [Coventry] up 2 Divs in 5 years
- First all-seater stadium for Cov.
- Introduced 3 points for a win to the World via the Football League
- Dunc [sic], Alison, Graham, Joanna, Jamie [his five children]
- First professional player to introduce and opinionate, as TV critic to front a programme from start to finish
- Introduced pre-match entertainment before League matches at Cov.
- 1st pro player to become a Football League member
- Won Hobbs bat, 31 N.O. [not out], at age of 8
- Rode start of Grand National course
- Founder member of SPARKS* charity
- Wrote and promoted 1st club song [for Coventry]
- Wrote 'Arsenal' song
- Only ex-professional player to be manager, director, managing director, chairman.

*SPARKS is the charity closest to Jimmy's heart, and in 1960, he, Jim Laker (England cricketer in the Fifties), Dai Rees (one of Britain's leading golfers of the time) and Wally Barnes (Welsh footballer, played for Arsenal) started the charity; Jimmy is the sole surviving founder member. All active sportsmen, they felt the need for an organisation which would fund medical research so that children could be as fortunate as they had been (i.e. born without problems, able to take part in games and lead a normal, healthy life). They created the acronym based on 'Sport Aiding Research into Crippling Diseases for Kids', now known more simply as SPARKS.

To have succeeded at a few of those is remarkable; to have been instrumental in all of them is exceptional. He was perhaps most proud of the fourth on the list: being the highest living goal scorer in an away League match, where he earned the title of 'The Bearded Wonder'.

On Saturday, 15 March 1958 the *Star* reported:

Fulham took the lead after only five minutes at Doncaster. Macedo [Tony] saved twice in early Doncaster rushes. Then Chamberlain [Trevor, 'Tosh'] passed to Cook [Maurice], who scored with a cross shot from a sharp angle. Haynes [Johnny] and Cook harassed the Doncaster defence, but the home forwards hit back and Fulham defenders had plenty to do. Chamberlain cut in but McIntosh [Dave] smothered his shot. After 20 minutes Chamberlain centred and McIntosh pushed the ball out but Hill scored from short range. After 20 minutes Fulham were three up, Hill scoring again. Hill tested McIntosh with a cross shot, but Haynes, Cook and Hill switched places frequently. Within a few minutes of resuming [after half-time] Fulham were four up. Stapleton [Joe] put the ball out to Haynes, who put it back into the middle, and Hill raced on to score. Fulham went further ahead after 52 minutes Hill getting his fourth goal. He scored his fifth in the 59th minute.

Jimmy said in the *Daily Mail* two days later on 17 March 1958, 'I never scored more than two League goals before,' and a journalist in *Soccer Star* wrote admiringly, 'Jimmy Hill is a player of gargantuan stature both in physique and heart.'

One incident he failed to include occurred at a match at Highbury on 16 September 1972 when Arsenal were at home to Liverpool. During the first half Dennis Drewitt, one of the linesmen, pulled a muscle in his leg so severely that he had to be carried off and, in accordance with FA rules, a match must have one referee and two linesmen or the game cannot continue. An announcement was made over the loudspeaker system, the soccer equivalent of, 'Is there a doctor in the house?' asking if there was anyone able to take his place. Jimmy, a fully qualified referee, made his presence known – a gesture which was ridiculed by the press. This assumption that he had leapt out of his seat riled him considerably, and he had the chance to put the record straight in an interview for *beebChat* in 1998, as is evident in the following transcript:

> I didn't offer my services immediately but it appeared that, after a few minutes or so, they couldn't find anyone competent, so I made my way down to the dressing room and offered to take the line. Pat Partridge the referee said, 'You'll do me Jimmy, get changed!'

With a crowd of over 47,000 ready for the game to continue, play was held up for nearly fifteen minutes while kit was found for Jimmy to wear, but all they could rustle up at such short notice was a mismatched tracksuit and a pair of size eight trainers. Jimmy takes large tens. In spite of his feet being crammed into such small boots, painfully crushing his toes, he struggled on until half-time, when he changed into a pair his size.

Bob Wilson, Arsenal's goalkeeper, recalls in his autobiography:

> Jimmy took some stick from the crowd every time he raised his flag but he never seemed to worry about what people thought of him.... . Once we ran a series of BBC Sport road shows around the country where we met the fans. At Maine Road, Manchester he turned up late and was booed or heckled throughout the entire evening, but he still made them laugh as well. Laughter was always around the corner if you were in Jim's company. At Goodison Park while covering the match for the BBC, we needed to make our way from the dressing room

area to the main camera gantry. Jimmy insisted we walk around the cinder track surrounding the pitch. From the moment he appeared boos rang out and toffees were thrown at him, but his response was typical saying 'I told you they loved me!' followed by a wink and a grin.

With an unfathomable belief in fairness and justice Jimmy has stormed up some strange and winding paths One of the major initiatives for which he is probably best known, and which had the biggest effect on football in this country (and is still argued about today), was when he spearheaded the campaign to abolish the maximum wage for players. I can't count how often I heard him pontificate, 'I've always believed that players should be paid what they can earn. Why should football be different from any other business?'

It is worth remembering that, post war, interest in the 'working man's ballet' had exploded. As a small lad Jimmy used to go to Fulham's home games with his father, and when they were playing away, they switched to Stamford Bridge to watch Chelsea. Men in those days never left the house without some sort of headgear, and when a goal was scored every hat and cap was thrown into the air in jubilation, which created a lottery, with the lucky few going home with the same hat they had set out with.

Although attendances increased considerably across the nation at all levels of the game, players' salaries had not. At the top end you had the likes of Stanley Matthews, Tom Finney and Nat Lofthouse providing Saturday-afternoon theatre alongside the burgeoning European Club competition, which was beginning to gather momentum. Each club throughout the Football League would have its own terrace heroes who not only entertained but attracted local support in record numbers through cash-rich turnstiles, but there was a growing deep sense of injustice and anger among players to end the relatively derisory sums they believed they were earning. Many top players went abroad to seek their fortune. The Football League argued that footballers earned 25% more than the average £16 weekly wage received by miners. The players retaliated, in particular with a speech from Bolton's Tommy Banks, who responded at a Professional Footballers' Association (PFA) meeting in Manchester that although many of the players could work down the mines, it was uncertain how many miners could play in front of 30,000 spectators.

The wage ceiling was one of two concerns. The other was the retain-and-transfer system, which gave the clubs complete authority regarding player osmosis from one club to another. Together, the two matters prompted a player strike (for the first time in history) scheduled for 21 January 1961. Public animosity grew as threats came from both sides – so much so that the 'pools companies, preparing for the worst, went to the lengths of producing two coupons for that weekend's fixtures.

When Jimmy, 'a forceful wing-half', was playing for Brentford (1949–52), Ron Greenwood was captain of the team. This is how Ron recounts Jimmy's appointment as Players' Union delegate in his autobiography, *Yours Sincerely Ron Greenwood* (CollinsWillow, 1984): '"You're an intelligent lad," I said to him, "You can be Players' Union representative and collect the subs. Nobody else wants the job!"'

Although not a political animal, Jimmy took on the role once again at Fulham in 1956 at the age of 27. In his autobiography *The Jimmy Hill Story* (Hodder & Stoughton, 1998) he writes:

Norman Smith, whose task it was to collect the subs and attend meetings, decided to take up a career in accountancy and, as a result, resigned from his Union responsibilities. Since I had done the job at Brentford I was made favourite to take over at Fulham. Needless to say there was not a queue but I was quite happy to help, not realising for one moment that it would mean anything more than a couple of meetings a year and collecting the subscriptions.

At the time it didn't promise to be time-consuming or demanding but it turned out to be a decision which would change my life and thrust me into a public battle as a young man which would alter the face of football as well as my own future. In 1960 I was already in my second two-year term as chairman of the Professional Footballers' Association. I had persuaded the committee to dispense with the name of Players' Union and give our title the somewhat superior status of a professional body of people – snobbish if you like but it did no harm to the cause we were fighting. The conclusive meeting started at 2.30 p.m. and at 6.20 p.m. the strike was off as a result of an agreed seven-point plan solely to facilitate a fair and legal formula to operate at the end of a player's contract. The vital clause was Number 7, which said 'If by 31 August he is still not transferred, the management committee of the Football League will, on the application of the player, deal with the matter.' The player in dispute would be paid throughout, although only a minimum wage of £15/14/13/12 per week, depending on which division, from 30 June to 31 July.

The contracted maximum wage during the playing season was just £20 per week and had been since the late 1950s, and prior to that, the maximum was £15 per week, which was installed in the 1952–53 season. Three days before the planned strike, after lengthy discussions with the football authorities, Jimmy announced a strike had been avoided as the Football League gave in to the players' demands. Alongside Jimmy were the PFA secretary Cliff Lloyd, a quiet, determined gentleman, and solicitor George Davies, who made a formidable back-up team, dotting the 'i's and crossing the 't's behind his buccaneering leadership. Jimmy was recognised as a master negotiator against the elder statesman of the football establishment, who were seen as being oppressive and out of touch. 'Hill's finest hour' was the headline the following day, and he was portrayed in the press as a working-class hero. The alterations to the players' contracts heralded monumental changes to football in general, and to footballers individually.

The London meeting on 18 January 1961 was held at the Ministry of Labour, and by the time Jimmy came out of it, the decision had been made. He wrote:

Two points arose: first, a player would still lose the difference between a minimum wage and his contract wage during the month of July. Secondly, the phrase 'deal with the matter' was key. It was understood to mean 'get the player moved' subject to a reasonable transfer fee being paid to his club. As I sat reading the newspapers the following day, I was a very happy man. It seemed as if English football had turned the corner. No further need for players to go to Colombia or Italy, except on holiday, which they may now be able to afford, and the competition would surely raise the standard at home.

They were prophetic words, and five years later (in 1966) England beat Germany in the final of the World Cup. This may have been coincidental, given that the tournament was held on home turf, but there were other strong reasons for such a triumph: the England squad was one of exceptional talent, they were managed by Sir Alf Ramsey, the 'feel good' factor had increased around dressing rooms up and down the country and, of course, everything was swinging in the Sixties. Most importantly, the restrictive shekel-capped shackles were off and players could begin to improve their skills, talents and professionalism in their chosen career path knowing they would be rewarded without constraints being imposed on their contracts.

Representing the players as the PFA Chairman, a relatively young Jimmy Hill took on the footballing establishment and played them off the park. Not a Rooney or a Ronaldo, a Beckham or a Best, a Cantona or a Charlton could have earned as much without this landmark change to players' contracts. There cannot be one player over the last half a century (or his agent) having signed a professional football contract who isn't in some way indebted to Jimmy's leadership all those years ago.

In a letter dated 17 February 1957 to a Fulham grocer addressed simply as 'Harry', Jimmy states clearly his feelings regarding players' wages: 'I would dearly love to see the status of a professional soccer player raised but I am afraid it can only be done by them picking themselves up by their own feet.'

Jimmy was none too impressed by an article on the subject proffered by Rob Hughes in *The Times* which appeared on Boxing Day 1994, entitled 'A Game in Grave Need of Goodwill'. It provoked an instant reply to the editor:

I appreciate a writer's [i.e. Rob Hughes'] license at this time of the year to delve into the world of pantomime and fantasy. Whilst 'pontificating' on television or reflecting on the past, perhaps I pursue the truth to a point where it upsets others. On recalling the happenings at the Ministry of Labour on 18 January 1961, as Max Boyce might point out, 'I was there'. Whilst not wishing to decry one who can no longer answer back, a touch of truth about the part Alan Hardaker played in the final negotiations to end the maximum wage would surely not go amiss in a newspaper of the stature of *The Times*. The protracted negotiations were at last coming to a conclusion. The right of a player to leave a club at the end of a contract it seemed had been accepted. Yet, in writing to the clubs on the next day to confirm this section of the agreement, the Secretary of the Football League subtly – but significantly – changed its wording to the extent that the clubs were led to believe that the principle had not been conceded. Thus it took the Eastham case three years later and the law of the land, enforced by Lord Justice Wilberforce, to repair that mischievous damage. However, it is in assessing Mr Hardaker's role in the (no maximum) issue that Rob Hughes wears somewhat tinted glasses. The 'no maximum' wage, the second principle for which the players had been prepared to go on strike, had clearly been conceded. Because a maximum wage did not exist in Italy, as well as in many other footballing nations, it would inevitably end sooner or later in this country. Nevertheless, having won that freedom on that historic afternoon we offered a practical olive branch across the table: notably to cushion such a dramatic change, we were prepared to accept a maximum wage providing an unrestricting performance bonus could be paid on results individually or collectively at the end of the season. Thus the carrot would be in the right place in relation to the donkey. 'You've got what you wanted. Be satisfied with that!' came the devastating riposte from the other side of the table. Today's players and managers for that matter should know who to thank.

Despite it being a bank holiday, I had to exchange my paper party hat for a more than skew-whiff secretarial one and had the onerous duty of typing and sending the letter to the editor Richard Sachs. I added an apologetic *post scriptum*: 'Further to our telephone conversation this afternoon, here is Jimmy's letter again, just in case my first faxing (on Boxing Day – need I say more???) didn't get through!'

Johnny Haynes played alongside Jimmy at Craven Cottage as inside forward. Probably Fulham's greatest player, he won 56 England caps and was the first footballer to receive the life-changing sum of £100 a week. Ironically, in a mischievous twist of fate, Jimmy never earned more than £20, having had to retire due to knee injuries shortly before the laws were changed.

3

Jolly Good Sports

A player shall not wear anything which is dangerous to another player.
—*The Laws of the Game.* Law 4 – Players' Equipment

Jimmy's first sporting attempts were to the evocative aestival sound of the crack of leather on willow when, as a little boy, he would go and watch his stepsister Rene play cricket. With adulthood, when football took over his life the bat wasn't banished to gather dust at the back of the wardrobe. Tom Wilson, his old friend from Fulham days, ended his professional footballing career in 1966 as captain of Folkestone Invicta FC. Tom made many friends at the Kent club and wanted to keep a connection going. Although he played football professionally for those two clubs his big love was cricket and, acquainted with many people from that world, he was inspired to get a group together (mostly from Hampshire, where he was living at the time) to go to Folkestone where the home team 'would thrash them'.

A wandering side with no base, the Hampshire Stragglers, as they became known, comprised legends such as Denis Compton CBE (MCC, Middlesex, England – Jimmy admired Denis, who could eat his way through a wing of fried skate including the bones) and Godfrey Evans CBE (Kent, England). Tom subsequently persuaded Jimmy to form his own XI of 'celebs', including Angus 'Gus' Fraser MBE (Middlesex and England – Jimmy: 'I taught him everything he knows'), to play against the Stragglers at Petersfield, after which there would be a thumping good meal and old-fashioned singsong, which drifted on well into the night.

Peter Alliss (the voice of televised golf par excellence) told me:

It is said the busiest people have the most time. That's certainly my experience of a 35-year friendship with Jimmy Hill. It was his love of golf that initially brought us together and at his peak he was a very good man to have on your side. I suppose it was his enthusiasm that first excited me. It didn't matter what he was tackling, it was always going to work and everything would be OK. He truly was a renaissance man. He was elegant, charming, a hard worker, nobody's fool. When I was on the Professional Golfers' Association Committee and we were looking for a new secretary I thought: Jimmy Hill. Although he was steeped in the world of football, he could have done the job. He had foresight, could see problems and had the knack of sorting them out. He had style. I wish we had a few Jimmy Hills around today – a rare talent – someone who could sit on any committee, covering any subject and make a contribution. Quite remarkable.

4

Fun and Games with Raquel Welch

Karl Fisher has cut the Hill hair for years and he has been a huge support to me since Jimmy's illness and the dearest of friends. Back in the Sixties, Karl worked at Robert Fielding's salon in Sloane Street in London. One day he had an appointment with an American woman who explained she was working on a film and needed a hairdresser for the new actress they were grooming. The young starlet came to the salon as planned. A short time later an appointment was made for a Mrs Curtis. When she arrived to see Karl, to his surprise and admiration the butterfly had emerged from the chrysalis: Mrs Curtis had become the larger-than-life superstar Raquel Welch.

At the bottom of a drawer among a load of press cuttings I found these notes written by Jimmy in 1972 when Raquel was back in London to promote another film:

Thursday 10.30 Arrive at studios to witness interview between Raquel Welch and Dickie Davies for World of Sport. Aware of no bra – on Raquel of course – pull stomach in.

10.40 Meet Miss Welch's PR man who asks me to arrange with the Sportsman Club to hold a press conference on the following day. I fix and report to PR man, who points out that Raquel Welch is not expecting to be photographed by the 25 photographers present, who are expecting to photograph her. Reason, no one has yet told her they are there. Sense trouble.

11.00 Interview finished. Miss Welch charming, smiling, beautiful. I enter studio and am introduced as TV executive. A friend points out I am an old pro (footballer). Miss Welch singularly unimpressed.

11.04 25 photographers walk through the door.

11.05 Raquel blows top (I'm on her side).

11.06 I leave for launch of new malt whisky at Sportsman Club.

11.08 Raquel bursts into tears in make-up room.

11.15 I taste splendid new malt whisky - recover confidence.

[In 1971, in his senior executive position at LWT, Jimmy headed the press campaign to promote the fledgling channel at the Monte Carlo Festival. On the team were Pauline Collins and John Alderton, who were yet to star in *Upstairs Downstairs*, and their friend, the New Zealand actress Nyree Dawn Porter. When Nyree played the part of Irene in BBC's production of *The Forsyte Saga* in 1967, practically the entire male population of the United Kingdom fell in love with her. Nyree had recently lost her husband, and Jimmy made sure she was looked after.

'Dearest Jimmy,' she wrote, 'I meant to ring you yesterday, but didn't have a second to spare, so I felt I must write and tell you how very much I enjoyed Derby Day. Incidentally, I hope that things are going smoothly at LWT for you'.

12.00 I am told Miss Welch and party are at the door and wish to see me.

12.02 Meet Raquel Welch and retinue of intimidated PR followers who have come to inspect the premises. Offer to taste new malt whisky declined politely. Proceed through happy whisky tasters to scrutinise facilities for Friday.

12.10 Commence walking discussion with Raquel - she's afraid to stand still in case she gets cornered. Suggest a microphone - she resists, walking away - wants it informal - point out informality a disadvantage if no one can hear. Suggest unobtrusive mike - she walks away again. 'Look', I say, 'do you really want to be professional?' She stops, turns and looks at me for the first time. 'Yes,' she said. 'Right, well stop walking around and sit down in that chair. Tell me exactly what you want in five minutes and that's what you'll get.' Astonished at effect of malt whisky. Expect press conference to be cancelled.

12.15 Hear Miss Welch say, 'That's what I like to hear - straight speaking - only sportsmen can do that.' Am astonished she remembered. She sits down and we prepare itinerary for conference.

12.25 Offer white wine (her favourite I'm told). She asks for champagne. Drinks one glass and goes.

12.30 Return to malt whisky and lunch with Hunter Davies.

Friday

Arrive at Sportsman for lunch and more malt whisky

2.30 Note absence of sporting journalists

2.45 Am alarmed at absence of sporting journalists

3.00 Panic

3.05 Arrange at short notice for Sportsman staff to impersonate sporting journalists. Collect Derek Ibbotson, Peter Lorenzo and others from lunch to fire questions.

3.10 Raquel arrives, scorns microphone. Pseudo journalists nearly give the game away by asking intelligent questions. Our heroine enchants the assembly for an hour but keeps asking where Chelsea team are. Explain footballers, like film stars, can be temperamental. Having had two invitations to meet cancelled, may be getting fed up.

4.20 Photograph with Mick McManus. Have some difficulty in preventing him wrestling with her.

5.00 Our guest leaves in buoyant mood expressing regret at not meeting Peter Osgood. I suggest catching later plane on Saturday and going to Chelsea v Leicester football match. Unfortunately, she must leave in morning. *Au revoir,* Miss Welch.

8.00 Receive message to telephone Raquel at Savoy.

8.02 Call Savoy. Raquel has cancelled plans and wants to go to Chelsea. Would I fix? Express delight – am onto scoop.

8.15 Set about arranging film unit to cover much-heralded meeting between Raquel and Peter Osgood [played for Chelsea and England]. Ring Bob Gardam's [television all-round wizard: directing/camera etc. at LWT] baby sitter. Her employer is attending a celebration of Old Elizabethans, regurgitating his school days.

8.15 Second telephone call reveals that Mike Archer [director, LWT], on his violin, is accompanying a parental *The Pirates of*

Penzance rendering at a school somewhere in the wilds of Hertfordshire.

8.19 Third time lucky – Mike Murphy at home – ready and willing to do anything to get to the top, including finding cameraman for tomorrow.

Saturday

Sunny, happy morning!

11.30 Order chauffeur driven limousine and proceed to Savoy to collect Raquel. Catch my breath at the impressive combination of style and beauty: outfit sensational if a touch daring weather-wise: a two-piece, light blue trouser suit of the finest suede, embracing a gossamer blouse. The trousers cling to the calves terminating at the ankles, above finely made (very expensive) high-heeled sandals.

11.45 My companion requests gum or sweeties. We stop at sweet shop and I buy a quarter of the stock. Weather still fine. At Stamford Bridge, Chairman Brian Mears greets us. 'Wine or champagne?' 'Champagne,' comes the answer.

12.02 Murphy arrives with cameraman. Introduce him as one of the most promising young film directors in London aware he has never directed a film in his life. Ossie [Peter Osgood] arrives. Raquel feigns a swoon. Murphy directs, cameraman points and superstars sparkle ...

12.30 Celebrate with more champagne, also sparkling.

1.30 Retire to Chelsea's only remaining stand 150 yards away. Sun disappears, wind horrific, rain torrential; Raquel's umbrella ineffective. Reach stand, climb two flights of concrete steps. Angel of mercy in form of Mrs Mears appears exercising enormous charm and tact. 'You *poor* darling!' Hands RW a mammoth brandy and they disappear into the Ladies' Room. I stage right into less volatile arms of Leicester City's chairman Len Shipman, and fellow directors.

2.30 Raquel and I take adjoining seats covered by *Big Match* cameras. Notice increase in warmth from 'Rocky' (pet name from those close to her ...) Grasp I'm alongside very proud mother of two. Hope she thinks I'm human, too. Sun shines again.

3.30 Raquel leaves while match is still in progress. From touchline she blows kiss to Ossie in goalmouth.

3.45 In car back to HQ at the Savoy, Miss Welch looks at me and says, 'Jim, how would you like to handle me in Europe?'

5

Channel Hopping

A player is in an off-side position if he is nearer to his opponent's goal-line than the ball, unless:
  a) He is in his own half of the field of play, or
  b) There are at least two of his opponents nearer their own goal-line than he is.

—*The Laws of the Game*. Law 11 – Off-side

Before I go any further I would like to confirm that I shall never, ever understand (and I know I am not alone) the whys and wherefores of the off-side rule. Help came when I saw this in one of Jimmy's scrapbooks from 1955:

Rules for 5-a-side Football (devised by the Central Council of Recreation):

1. Only the defending goalkeeper is allowed inside the goal area and he may handle the ball only in this area.

Penalty for Infringement: (a) By the defence – a penalty kick; (b) by the attack – a free kick at the point of entry to the circle.

Note – Accidental entry by a player into the goal area which has no effect on play is not penalised.

2. Apart from this rule, there is no offside.

The 5-a-side rules also state that each half only lasts for seven minutes, so an entire game (unless there is extra time, where 'play will continue until the first goal') won't last for more than 20 minutes. I reckon I could cope with that – just.

Jimmy actually began his broadcasting career behind the camera in 1968 as technical adviser for the BBC's football drama series *United!*

Filmed at Stoke City's ground, it starred George Layton (*Doctor in the House, Doctor at Large* and *Minder*) in the role of Jimmy Stokes and Stephen Yardley (*Howards' Way*) as Kenny Craig. It ran from 1965 to 1966 and was withdrawn after 147 episodes. Later that year Jimmy was appointed Head of Sport at London Weekend Television and, for a brief period until 1972, was Deputy Controller of Programmes. During the 1970 FIFA World Cup in Mexico (the first time the competition had been held outside Europe), Jimmy inspired the panel of football pundits.

On 27 November 1969 Barry Davies and Brian Moore provided the commentary and Jimmy acted as presenter for the first airing of *The Big Match* for Thames Television. He received a letter from the powers that be:

Well; that was a splendid first programme together. Why don't we direct each other again some day? I just want to thank you enormously for coming along and getting the show so neatly off the ground for us. Everybody seems to be very pleased with the whole thing – so that's alright!

The Big Match and its revolutionary panel proved a massively successful formula and he became hot property – so much so that the BBC cast its net to nick him. Two years later the Corporation succeeded, and issued this press release:

23 May 1973
BBC Television Press Office 17.45 p.m.
JIMMY HILL JOINS THE BBC

The BBC announced today that Mr Jimmy Hill has signed an exclusive contract for the next four years to appear as soccer analyst in its television sports programmes. His first appearances will be in BBC Television's live coverage of the European Cup Final between Ajax and Juventus next Wednesday 30 May, and the vital World Cup qualifying match between England and Poland, which the BBC is covering live on 6 June. Next season

Mr Hill will appear regularly in *'Match of the Day'* and other football programmes, and will be taking part in a new Friday evening sports review which BBC1 is to introduce in September. He will also take part in BBC Television coverage of the World Cup in West Germany next year. Bryan Cowgill, the BBC's Head of Sport and Outside Broadcasts, comments: 'We are delighted to welcome Jimmy to our television sports team and know that BBC viewers will enjoy his company on the screen as much as we will'. Mr Hill, 44, is a member of the Sports Council, a former chairman of the Professional Footballers Association, former Coventry City manager and an ex-Fulham and Brentford player. He comments: 'I am delighted to be returning to the BBC where I cut my teeth as a soccer analyst during the 1966 World Cup. What is particularly stimulating is the opportunity to be involved with a nationwide audience on a regular basis. I'm grateful for many happy years with London Weekend Television Sport, but I am now looking forward immensely to this new challenge to help develop television soccer coverage in the exciting years ahead.

On 28 May 1973 Bryan Cowgill sent this note of encouragement to his new presenter:

A brief but very sincere note of good wishes to you for Wednesday night and the start of what I know is going to be a great chapter for you and for us. You know how much we all look forward to it with professional anticipation and the greatest personal pleasure.

The BBC first started broadcasting in colour in 1966, but in 1973 not everyone benefited from the new technology, each programme going out both in black and white and in colour.

Jimmy received many telegrams and letters of congratulations when the news was released. Mike Archer (director, LWT) wrote:

I am now able to write having watched your first performance in monochrome from Tenby in South Wales. Congratulations.

Considering the lack of back-room talent you have obviously got to put up with, I thought you chaired the discussion very well. I rather think you were hurried into your vote for Juventus just before the kick-off – this really surprised me. Anyhow, apart from the fact that the BBC has obviously worn out its recording of the winning goal, I think you can be well satisfied.

Then there came an anonymous cable from the more fragrant army of fans: 'We also serve who only stand and wait. Congratulations. The Wives.'

The following is an extract from the survey after the first broadcast on 25 August 1973 from the Audience Research Department, dated 14 September 1973:

1. Size of audience (based on results of the Survey of Listening and Viewing). It is estimated that the audience for this broadcast was 15% of the United Kingdom population. Programmes on BBC2 and ITV at the time were seen by 4.7% and 11% (averages).

2. Reaction of audience (based on 135 questionnaires completed by 11% of the viewing panel)
   A+ 13%, A 35%, B 44%, C 7%, C− 1%
   This gives the reaction index of 63.

3. The return of *Match of the Day* was welcomed and this first programme featuring league football (as opposed to last week's Watney Cup Final) was generally enjoyed. The matches feature contained some good and exciting football, it was agreed and the commentaries by John Motson and – particularly – Barry Davies proved helpful and, by and large, unobtrusive, although there were a few who obviously felt that all television commentators tended to talk too much, forgetting that the viewers could see for themselves what was happening. Several thought it a good idea to ask Barry Davies to comment later in the programme on his own commentary on the Derby v Chelsea clash. Although, also with regard to this match, one group felt it unnecessary – undesirable even – to show the violence on the terraces.

Occasional viewers complained of too many slow-motion replays and not enough of the actual football.

4. Asked what they thought of Jimmy Hill, views in the sample replied as follows:

Exceptionally good: 22%

Quite good: 66%

Poor: 12%

Clearly, there was quite a marked division of opinion here. Some, for instance, very much admired his approach: as an ex-professional himself, he 'knew the game inside out', it was remarked, and his informed comments and incisive match analysis made him a great asset to any football pro-gramme. There were, nevertheless, quite a few complaints that he had far too much to say and that the 'new style' *Match of the Day* seemed overloaded with enquiries, post mortems, etc. at the expense of football itself.

5. 90% watched it all, 2% came in the middle, 2% tried a bit and 6% switched off before the end.

The year 1974 saw the publication of *Jimmy Hill's Football Review* in which he confesses: 'I shall never forget my first programme for the BBC after signing a contract with them for four years. I won't forget it because I sat for the whole of the two hours with the most excruciating stomach ache one could imagine.'

And in another article he admitted:

Since the first day I was taken away to play in what I thought was to be my first Football League game I have always slept badly on the night before a big occasion. That first day was when, as a professional player for Brentford we travelled to play Bradford Park Avenue. I was sure I was in the team and lay in my bed all night long, hearing the trains shunting up and down Bradford Station – and I swear I didn't get a wink of sleep. I was in a similar condition so many years later the night before my BBC debut. Apart from being at the top of their profession you couldn't meet two more pleasant people than Ron Greenwood and Jock Stein. They are the most sympathetic of friends one could lean upon in times of trouble. I was very glad to have them with me on this particular occasion. I said to both of them before the programme, 'Stay with me lads especially during the early moments and I promise I will come back to life and be myself within a very short time'. As I remember it the game was not a classic but, rather unusual for me, most of the details disappeared with my stomach pain. What I do remember, both Jock and Ron were in great form when discussing the game at halftime and the end of the match. Their joint knowledge of European football is unsurpassed and I could feel the points that they were making were interesting me and I knew they must be going home with the audience.

It is true that the camaraderie between Ron and Jimmy was as good as any. In his autobiography Ron spoke of their time at Brentford, which instigated 'a close and enduring friendship'. He continued:

Jimmy has always known that if he is in trouble he can call on me. I will not have a bad word said about him. He has a streak of independence, which means he will always be his own man. It is one of the reasons he has achieved so much. He can be counted on when it matters.

'There is a moment when an interviewee or panellist is flowing freely,' Jimmy continues, referring still to Ron and Jock, 'where it is possible to relax fractionally and just rest a moment to evaluate how things are going. They were in such good form they provided me with much needed breathing space.'

I was always under the impression that Jimmy had nerves of steel. However, like the proverbial swan, all appears calm above water but in Jimmy's case all hell was being let loose in the engine room below. Jimmy confessed to a second weakness in the 2004 BBC publication *40 Years of Match of the Day* by Martyn Smith:

One of the biggest changes I found when I joined the BBC was Autocue. Everything I had done at LWT had been as a pundit and I was able to speak off the top of my head. I used it for the first time on my very first show but I was never a great script reader. Before, I'd been an ad-libber and just hoped that I was alright. To suddenly read out loud was difficult at first but I soon got used to it and was professionally adequate in a short space of time.

The second performance was rather different. The match we were going to cover was Poland v England from Katowice [a city in the south of the host nation]. The panellists were Bob Wilson and the man himself, Brian Clough. I had fewer nerves, but still some such was the importance of the match for all those of us dying for England to qualify for the World Cup. Brian came into the studio oozing confidence. 'The Poles were a bunch of amateurs,' he declared saying that England would have no difficulty in beating them by at least three goals. Bob wasn't as sure and took a bet of ten pence to that effect. I was too busy worrying about professional responsibilities to make a forecast but I was sure England wouldn't be beaten. At half-time, with England one goal down, Brian was still confident that it would be plain sailing in the second half and, although expecting slightly rougher course, Bob and I thought that England had played well enough to get that goal back and, at least, earn a draw.

When England tragically lost the second goal after a suc-cessful tackle by Lubanski on Bobby Moore, we all began to get worried. Brian took what looked to be a crazy bet of 10p with Bob – probably in order to get his money back – that Alan Ball would be sent off before the end of the game. Well, you know the result: Alan was sent off, England lost, Brian and Bob lost no money, but it was the prelude to England losing its place in the World Cup Finals. I was particularly pleased that in a brief personal analysis I was able to reveal that the way in which Moore had been robbed of the ball was not just an accident. I had felt that the Poles had positively set out to pressurise Bobby using quick players like Lubanski to get in, tackle him, unsettle him and maybe rob him and produce the goals that they so desperately needed. It wasn't until four days later in the Sunday papers that the Polish coach revealed just that.

Yet I was more pleased that night with the discussions that took place off the 'air'. I suppose we were in Lime Grove Studios for as long as four hours – and when footballers are together they mostly talk about football.

During my research I came across a curious bundle, every millimetre of paper covered in columns of figures. Handwritten by ex-RAF Wing Commander Charles Reep and dated 19 July 1974 (following the World Cup Final), the ink was faded, the script so small and neat, as if written by an ant, that it proved difficult to read. An amateur statistician, Wing Commander Reep was fascinated by the number of passes played that led to a goal. Known for his 'long ball theory', later taken up by Charles Hughes and Graham Taylor (when managing the England team) these notes, however madcap and off the wall they appeared to an ignoramus like me, made for fascinating reading. West Ham's manager Sam Allardyce is currently an exponent of the principle, as is Aloysius 'Louis' van Gaal at Manchester United.

At least eight matches and preferably 12 are required for a reliable indication of average ratios. Holland's goal-shot ratio [during the 1974 World Cup Finals] is probably flattering (15 goals, 106 shots), between 1 in 8 and 9 being probably the true figure. But Brazil's goal-shot ratio for the six matches (3 goals, 73 shots) is so bad that the true average would also be bad. All figures indicate that West Germany, Poland and Holland were fairly evenly matched and only random chance decided West Germany should be the winners. West Germany had a 'freak' win over Poland, but also had an almost 'freak' defeat by East Germany, 0-1. In the final, West Germany and Holland 'earned' a draw [West Germany beat the Dutch 2-1]. Of the apparent failures, Italy and Scotland were probably as good as West Germany, Poland and Holland, potentially.

I wonder what Mr Clough would have said had he been in possession of a crystal ball?

In a promotion for the new football season the *Radio Times* ran a four-page spread by John Sandilands entitled 'The Sporting Life of Jimmy Hill'.

> He [Jimmy] belongs in the classic mould of those sporting heroes beloved of boys' comics like *Wizard* and *Hotspur*: those paragons who dealt so masterfully with every challenge put before them. He is tall and broad-shouldered with the authentic spring in his step and his eyes are astoundingly clear and healthy. Even his hawk nose and indomitable jaw-line are gifts to the artists who brought such Titans alive.

During the interview Jimmy paused to make a telephone call in order to fix up a game of tennis the next day at the Hurlingham Club. Who was his partner in crime? A young 17-year-old Swede, 'the most outstanding new player of the year', called Björn Borg.

Jimmy was never afraid of raising an issue, however confrontational it might be. In a letter from Sam Leitch [Head of Sport], it was clear he had objected to the duration of *Sportswide*:

> I don't want to add to your worries nor take up your limited time unnecessarily but I would like to make the gentlest of formal protests about *Sportswide*. You will remember that when I was invited to join the BBC, my participation in a national, virile Friday night sports programme was as much a part of the package as my involvement with *Match of the Day*.
>
> At the time we were all thinking in terms of a half hour programme as an entity and fronted by me. It hasn't turned out like that. My concern is that, because of the structure of Friday night programmes, *Sportswide* tends to get used as a piece of scheduling elastic. Whether it's elections, bombs, Christmas programmes, lengthy films or as just happened, *Sportstown* not being made or cut to the right length, it is always *Sportswide* which bears the brunt.

Sam replied:

> I appreciate how keen you feel about *Sportswide* and the fact that it is as important to you as *Match of the Day*. Both are

highly successful in the sense that they produce between them a regular 20 million viewers weekly. And while you are not complaining about the transmission timing of *Sportswide* I think we all agree that at no other time on Friday night, even with a longer programme transmission, could there be an average audience of 8 million. The *Nationwide* set-up is neither comfortable nor convenient. But I also accept that this is not the source of your restrained irritation.

Therefore you have my assurance that following the two or three minutes' enforced reduction in the next two *Sportswides* the duration will be restored to not less than what we promised – 15 minutes.

On a lighter note, with Jimmy nearly always flying by the seat of his pants he once conducted his piece for *Sportswide* wearing jodhpurs (having had no time to change after his weekly ride) and a Sunday broadcast of *Match of the Day* in sheepskin slippers. He also used to light up his pipe in the studio when off camera ...

The competition between the BBC and ITV continued. On 5 February 1975 Jonathan Martin (BBC Head of Sport) sent out a blind copy to Jimmy of the *Match of the Day* audience figures:

I know the recent *Match of the Day* figures have not escaped your notice, but at this stage of the season I thought you would like to have a more detailed breakdown. Up to 25 January there have been 25 *Match of the Day* programmes, with a total audience of 227.5 million viewers, and a weekly average of 9.1 million. A breakdown of the last ten programmes, starting on 23 November reveals an average audience of 10.2 million, while the last six programmes from the Saturday before Christmas, have attracted a total audience of 63.5 million views, which gives us an average of 10.6 million.

'Jim,' Jonathan added in his own hand, 'the recent figures have included several 11.5 millions – the lowest in the last six weeks is 9.5!!!'

Match of the Day scooted from strength to strength, prompting the following compliment from Alan Hart (Controller of Programmes at the BBC, 1981-84): 'I thought that your contribution to Saturday was excellent, and helped both programmes go like a bomb. Good words, good perception, and good interviews.'

'I loved being part of *MOTD*,' Jimmy told Martyn Smith 'and am proud that by using my experience to give it a special perspective I was able to help bring something unique to the screen. For me it is a British institution without which Saturday nights are never the same.'

As if he didn't have enough on his plate, in the run-up for the Queen's Silver Jubilee celebrations in 1977 Jimmy was called upon yet again for his advice and help and headed the sports committee as chairman and was awarded a medal for his contribution.

Jimmy received many letters not only from the general public but also from those involved in the world of football, and one from Stan Cullis (manager of Wolverhampton Wanderers 1948-1964, and Birmingham City 1965-1970) dated September 1978 caught my eye:

Your brief analysis of the Denmark v England game 'hit the nail exactly on the head'. I have been aware of the lack of pace in the back four for some time. Developing the technical ability to turn quickly when an opponent takes you on, when I joined the Wolves as manager [as a raw recruit in 1934 he rose quickly in the ranks and became club captain], my manager, Major Buckley, gave me early lessons on the movement of the feet to acquire the skill. (1) The movement of a dancer on the dance floor, sliding along the floor in different directions – he performed the pirouetting around the gym to demonstrate. (2) The feet movements of a boxer in the ring who has to change his stance continually to keep perfect balance, having his opponent squarely in front of him at all times. I had to compensate for my ungainly speed by acquiring the knack of turning when the opponent 'took me on'. I practised the routines on my own for hours on end.

6

I Get to Meet the Man

At the beginning of the game, choice of ends and the kick-off shall be decided by the toss of a coin. The team winning the toss shall have the option of choice of ends or the kick-off.
—*The Laws of the Game.* Law 8 – The Start of Play

After nearly five years living in France I found it tough slotting back into an English groove, and picking up the threads with old acquaintances proved even harder, since most had moved on. I registered with several employment agencies, working as a temp in order to keep some money coming in, but even when I managed to be given full-time employment, a worrying pattern began to emerge, with each position ending almost before it began, through (I like to believe) no fault of my own.

On a wet morning in August 1976 I found myself, at the age of 25, once again on the scrap heap of the great unemployed. I purchased a copy of *The Times* and, it being a Wednesday, turned to the *crème de la crème* page – the elite 'situations vacant' section. One ad jumped out at me:

'BBC TV SPORTS PERSONALITY WITH DOG SEEKS SUPER EFFICIENT PA'

I cannot abide sport, my typing is rusty and my shorthand non-existent – but I am a dog's best friend. How was I to know that on the day I bought that broadsheet my life would change forever? 'Sports personality with dog,' I read again. I was already on the books of that particular agency, and dialled their number.

'Why didn't you call me?'

'We were under the impression you wanted a busy office with lots of people. This is working from home.'

'Okay, fair enough, but who are we talking about?'

'Jimmy Hill.'

43

'Who?'

'You know. Him. *Match of the Day*. Beard? Football?'

I was getting fed up with trudging to countless interviews ranging from fruit importers in Spitalfields to anonymous conglomerates within the Square Mile. One agency arranged a rendezvous at the Cumberland Hotel, Marble Arch, with an exotic-looking foreign gentleman with long, greasy hair, a startlingly white suit with matching teeth like china cups, and Cuban-heeled boots. Minutes into the meeting he invited me to go for a spin in his convertible vintage American car; I declined politely and made a speedy exit.

My longest period of employment was with the British Agricultural Export Council in Knightsbridge working as PA for the Chief Executive, Major John Thorneloe, a gentle giant of a man who, on retiring from the Army, farmed in Oxfordshire. His youngest child and the apple of his eye, Lt-Col Rupert Thorneloe MBE, was killed in action in Helmand Province, Southern Afghanistan on 1 July 2009, the most senior British officer to have died out there. Recently we have been in touch, as I wanted him to know that I mention his son in this book. In reply to my email, he wrote:

> It was wonderful to receive your email, despite the sad news regarding Jimmy. You are so good and an example to all who wish to be positive despite setbacks not of their own making. How very kind of you to include Rupert in your 'Jimmy' book. He would be a General now according to General Dannatt [Chief of the General Staff], had he not told one of his soldiers to change places with him so that he was 'Top Cover' in his tank/ armoured car. The other day I looked him up on Google and I was astounded regarding the amount of information about him and things I never knew. He was the epitome of modesty.

I asked the agency to arrange an interview. They fixed a date but told me that Mr Hill was abroad on business and I would be seeing his girlfriend Veronica. I took the tube to Notting Hill Gate and found their mid-terrace house down a quiet street off the Bayswater Road.

A tall, attractive girl a few years my senior opened the front door, clutching an elderly miniature poodle. She chivvied me into her

Jimmy's first sporting attempts with
leather and willow

From little acorns... Henry Thornton School
First XI, Jimmy aged 16, front row,
second from right

Right: a good enough trumpeter to play in
Johnny Dankworth's band

Showing hidden talents at the Boys' Brigade summer camp, 1941

A budding domestic god

The Brentford squad, Jimmy front row, second from right

The FA London XI on their way to play the Berlin XI, Germany 1951.
Jimmy second row, far right

JIMMY HILL, LEFT HALF AND SKIPPER OF THE CRACK FULHAM OUTFIT, WAS BORN IN 1928. HE STARTED IN BIG FOOTBALL AS AN AMATEUR FOR READING IN 1949, BUT COULD NOT HOLD HIS PLACE ON THE TEAM. HE WAS THEN PLAYING AT INSIDE LEFT, AND SO HE SWITCHED OVER TO BRENTFORD, BUT IN HIS FIRST SEASON WAS ALMOST BARRACKED OUT OF FOOTBALL, BY THE BRENTFORD CROWD. HE KEPT PLUGGING AWAY HOWEVER, TOOK OVER AT LEFT HALF WITH ENORMOUS SUCCESS, FINALLY BEING TRANSFERRED TO FULHAM FOR £22,500. JIM IS A CONSTRUCTIVE PLAYER, WHO PACKS A FINE SHOT, AND IS OF INVALUABLE SUPPORT TO HIS FORWARDS WITH LONG OR SHORT PASSES OR DIRECT DRIBBLING BURSTS.

HU SEALY

On tour in the West Indies – 'Skipper of the crack Fulham outfit'

Fulham Football Club in the Fifties – Jimmy back row, third from right

Frolicking with Trevor 'Tosh' Chamberlain at the Cottage
© PA Images

A round with Johnny Haynes, the first £100 a week player – all thanks to Jimmy
© Action Photos by H W Neale

On the way up – Jimmy having led Coventry City FC to win the
Third Division Championship, 1963-64 season

Getting ready with Brian Moore for the Big Match – Fulham v Plymouth
© Ken Coton

Raquel Welch being taken under Jimmy's wing

Alec Stock, Tommy Trinder and Jimmy at the Cottage, March 1973
© Ken Coton

The 'Tower Bridge' double act, Jimmy and Bruce
© REX

A charity do at the Sportsman club with Alan Pascoe

office and went downstairs to the kitchen to make us some coffee. Veronica asked lots of questions, after which I left for Sussex. The next day I was asked to come back the following Wednesday morning to meet Jimmy.

I hadn't a clue what to wear for my second interview and I wanted to make a good impression. Hoping I could get away with something casual (dresses in my wardrobe conspicuous by their absence), I polished my shoes, pulled on clean jeans and a Rosslyn Park sweatshirt, blissfully unaware that it referred to the wrong-shaped ball.

Veronica ushered me into the study where Jimmy, in contrast dressed smartly in a blue pinstriped suit, was sitting behind a large antique desk deep in conversation on the phone. I recognised him instantly, the overall picture being one of a dynamic, energetic man. I sat patiently, fascinated by the collection of framed photographs and pictures decorating the walls. There was a cartoon of him with Pope John Paul on the pitch at Wembley, a photo with Raquel Welch, several pictures of him swinging a golf club, and some with members of the royal family. Every now and then when he looked up, indicating he wouldn't be long, I was struck by his intelligent eyes. A further quarter of an hour later he put down the receiver and smiled apologetically.

'Sorry about that,' he said, 'Elton.'

He seemed affable and very laid back, and after we had been talking for nearly an hour, Veronica reappeared in the doorway.

'Chop, chop Jimmy. Meeting,' she said, tapping her watch.

When he stood up I was surprised to see, at six feet, how tall and slim he was. We shook hands, he said goodbye and wished me luck. Later that evening, I received a phone call asking when I could start.

On 23 September 1975 the *Daily Mail* ran a full-page spread written by – in many people's view the best-ever – British sports journalist Ian Wooldridge. Ian, who ended up working for the paper for half a century, was a good mate of Jimmy's and on the occasion of Woolers's (as he was known) 50th birthday in January 1982, we were invited to share in the celebrations at Scribes Club in central London. 'What can I give the old boy now that he's reaching retirement age?' Jimmy asked. Before I could reply, he said, 'Sheep-skin slippers and a pipe', his own favourite accessories.

Ian lived by the pen not the sword but, brave man that he was, he had experienced the high-octane adrenalin rush of running the bulls in Pamplona, once inveigling Jimmy to join him in the perilous chase. Miraculously they both survived, and Ian's article entitled 'It's the Jimmy Hill Show!' proves the strong friendship the two men shared.

Ian began the article with, 'One not uncommon denominator among ex-professional footballers is that they are incapable of long periods of sustained work. The stardom years convince them the world owes them a living, and the paternalistic nature of existence within the high walls of a major soccer club leaves them unequipped for the fierce reality outside. There are, of course, exceptions. Perhaps the most exceptional is an ex-Brentford and Fulham inside-right who never played for England.'

Ian had to stick with Jimmy for seven successive days and nights and, in order to do so, confessed he needed 'the constitution of a pneumatic driller, a digestive tract of galvanised steel, a talent for sleeping standing up and a capacity to breakfast off kippers and champagne when most of the human race would be heading for the nearest intensive care unit.'

Ian described the week (a typical one in the Hill household) as it panned out as follows: 'Sunday morning – charity [football] match (with England manager Don Revie)... even a downpour can't dampen the Fourth Form enthusiasm. The call on his parents [at his birthplace in Balham – "Jimmy gets his brains from his father and his personality from me"] stretches to four hours.'

Monday went as follows: 'By 9.00 a.m. he is working on the first of the 220 letters he will deal with in seven days. In that time he also has 139 incoming calls and 84 outgoing phone calls.' Next, Ian wrote, 'Jimmy has to leave for the HQ of Esso Petroleum to press a computer button which selects the winner of some competition, lunches in an executive suite, dashes home to collect enough clothes to outfit a repertory company, then heads up the M1 for the board meeting of Coventry [City Football Club].'

Ian then reports that, after having addressed the shareholders, his charge plays roulette in a casino until midnight, has dinner, and after only four hours' sleep, drives to Warwickshire on Tuesday morning to join the local hunt. Unfortunately Jimmy takes a tumble from his horse, landing heavily and painfully on his shoulder. Back home, safe but not sound, he changes 'rapidly behind the car and straight on to the next engagement – opening the golf range at Lord Aylestone's new leisure complex – with a speech and a ceremonial drive.'

On Wednesday the shoulder is too sore for him to take part in a charity golf tournament and instead Jimmy heads off for a meeting of the Sports Council and, in Ian's words, 'by mid-afternoon Hill is in the BBC studios preparing a script for the first of his three TV appearances of the week,' with 10 million viewers per programme.

The exhausting schedule continues: 'By Thursday Hill is sprinting to meetings with the Goaldiggers and the Football Association, with whose secretary, Ted Croker, he confers about sponsorship for next year's Home International matches.'

Jimmy manages to cram in a sandwich lunch at the Sportsman club for whom he is organising a charity dinner, then it's back to the BBC to discuss Friday's script. Next on the agenda is a meal with Gordon Milne and Eddie Plumley (both from Coventry City FC), which goes on until 2.30 a.m.

After Friday's programme Jimmy remains ensconced at the studio for a further two hours in discussion, followed by supper with friends and a relatively early bed. Next morning by 11.00 a.m. he is on a train to Manchester to watch United play Ipswich. Wearing his journalistic hat (Jimmy wrote a weekly article for the *News of the World*), after having dictated his comments over the phone, he is taken in a BBC car to the airport and, although the plane is delayed for 18 minutes, he has enough time to return to his house in Bayswater for a restorative bath, shampoo and dinner (which takes precisely 14 minutes) before going to the Lime Grove Studios, where they are, 'decidedly relieved to discover their programme presenter is still alive'.

How I wish I had had the opportunity to read Ian's article before I started working for Jimmy, as it would have given me some idea of what I was letting myself in for.

7

Arabian Knights

Not long before I arrived on the scene Jimmy had signed a contract with the Kingdom of Saudi Arabia to coach their national football team. In this transcript (translated in halting English by a Mr S. Hamade for the *Al-Jazeera* paper following a television interview), Jimmy reportedly announced:

'I have signed the contract with the President of Youth Welfare, not because I am merely a sport commentator, but a qualified athlete.' The English papers reported that you have received a large amount from the PYW. Now they call you 'Sheikh' or Senator Jimmy. Smiling he [Jimmy] said, 'the papers in question mentioned the amount in the contract is £25m, that amount is untrue, but a large amount is billed for stadia construction and another part goes to experts and coaches; therefore the English Press wrongly calculated that the whole amount would be paid to World Sports Academy [the company he created to deal with this particular consultancy business].'

It is known that you are a successful commentator who has a large number of audiences. Do you think that this success is linked to good planning on the sport level? He replied, 'I know that you ask me a kind question by which you mean that I am a broadcaster and being not qualified to have the position of WSA chairman. I wish to say to all people that my reputation as a commentator did not come gradually through the information section of sport so far as it is due to my long experience in football, which is my programme on British TV as well – the best I can produce is football training and administration. I am very pleased to return to football and work in the Academy.

The opportunity arrived when Jimmy was at the opening by HRH Prince Philip of the new headquarters of the National Playing Fields Association in Ovington Square near Knightsbridge. Jimmy chatted with another guest, an architect, who was involved in the construction of the Olympic village and stadium in Riyadh, about the merits of artificial grass playing surfaces.

In the *Daily Mail* on 14 March 1977 Jimmy said:

The Saudis had just taken part in the Arab games and finished third from bottom in the League, which wasn't a very good performance, and HRH Prince Faisal bin Fahad bin Adbul Aziz, the president of the Ministry of Youth Welfare, was unhappy about the bad results that the national team had achieved and was anxious to do something about it. When the architect was talking to him my name cropped up and Prince Faisal asked him if he would invite me to go to Saudi Arabia to discuss the problems of their football with him. That immediately sent me rushing for the map and the airline schedules. It was during my third visit that the Prince began to talk about me not only recommending what should be done but taking the responsibility of carrying it out. I said firmly that there was no way in which I wanted to take responsibility, because I had my contract with the BBC and my commitments in England in many fields, which would not enable me to live in Saudi Arabia. The Saudis don't easily take 'no' for an answer and, after a couple more visits, I was beginning to come round to the idea that perhaps if I could find the right man to run the operation in Saudi Arabia I could lead a double life.

Subsequently with Duncan (Jimmy's eldest son) appointed as General Manager, World Sports Academy had to recruit coaches, a physiotherapist and a full staff from the UK. His team included John Camkin (ex-journalist and director of Coventry City FC), Bill McGarry (ex-Wolves manager), David Woodfield (ex-Wolves centre-half), Geoff Vowden (ex-Nottingham Forest and Birmingham striker), John Birkett and John Manning, both prolific goal-scorers in the lower divisions.

The hothouse atmosphere in the Middle East, with all its restrictions and different way of life, did not suit everyone, and one such early casualty was David Icke. Having previously played in goal for Coventry City and then become a broadcaster for the BBC, he survived barely two months. In February 1977 David sent an apologetic letter in which he says he could not return to Saudi Arabia as he missed his wife and family too much.

He also wrote,

> There have been days in the last week when I have wanted to get back to Saudi's *Monty Python* world and leave behind the damp, depressing drabness that is the English winter.

When David referred to *Monty Python*, I don't know whether he had a clue that his boss had once appeared on the television programme in a sketch entitled 'The Queen Victoria Handicap', 'dressed as the monarch in crown, veil and all'.

8

Back to the Business in Hand

Under the terms of his contract, Jimmy flew out to Riyadh every month for a period of three days and, since it was necessary to obtain a separate visa for each trip, it was up to me to drop off the passport at the embassy. One Friday afternoon, Veronica said I could buzz off early for Sussex because she had to 'pack Jimmy's case for France'.

'France?' I gasped in horror. '*Abroad?*'

It was 4.30 p.m. and his passport lay buried in the consular section of the Saudi embassy. Veronica wasted no time and made a telephone call. Heaven knows how she did it, but she succeeded in persuading the officials that this was an emergency of national importance and they released the document. Jimmy, none the wiser, flew off to the sun the next morning to spend the weekend on the yacht of Sir Bernard Audley (chairman of JICTAR – Joint Industry Committee for Television Advertising Research), that was moored at Beaulieu-sur-Mer, while I had escaped a severe drubbing and, quite possibly, the sack.

Jimmy shared another secretary at the BBC to look after that side of things, and my duties included everything to do with his personal life; the countless charity commitments; consultancy and public appearances – above all, making sure he had the necessary paperwork for each appointment. I also dealt with correspondence and requests from the general public. When he was at home the atmosphere was manic. If the morning had been particularly busy Jimmy treated us to lunch at one of three local restaurants: either the smoky atmosphere of Russkie's wine bar opposite the Russian embassy, The Ark in Kensington Church Street or the cheap 'n' cheerful Pizza and Pasta on the Bayswater Road. Savile Row suits were banished and Jimmy opted for jeans, making him look years less than a few months short of his 49th birthday. He was used to the people coming up to him and saying, 'You look a lot younger in real life,' to which he would reply, 'then you must have a very old television set!'

The phone never stopped ringing and I had a great deal of difficulty in mastering the keyboard with several incoming lines (a task made increasingly difficult if we had shared a bottle of wine over lunch), and it didn't take long for Jimmy to rumble that I would never be able to keep up to speed with dictation.

He was captain of the Variety Club of Great Britain Golfing Society that year, and I came across an official list of raffle prizes for one of the dinners on the back of which Jimmy had written some bullet points under the heading of 'Managers' in preparation for a speech that he was to make during the evening:

Matt [Busby] - Background - charm - cunning - personality - experience
Revie [Don] - Intelligence - thoroughness - thoughtfulness to the 'nth degree
Shankly [Bill] - Experience - personality - humour.

Between the last two, Revie and Shankly, he had written: 'driving wife' - but I'm not sure to whom he was referring!

The list continues:

Paisley [Bob] - Experience - disguises cunning humour - teamwork
Alf [Ramsey] - Fanaticism - remote from players - kept distance - tactician - genius - Ipswich - pedigree: arrogance - loyalty
Clough [Brian] - Fanatic - frightening - distance - young men never boring
Greenwood [Ron] - Coach - passing-on technique - distance
Robson [Bobby] - Single mindedness - sound tactical sense - courage - passion.

Bernard Cribbins OBE remembers when the Lord's Taverners charity went on a golf trip to the West Indian paradise of Tobago. He, Tim Brooke-Taylor, Bruce Forsyth and Jimmy were in the party along with other worthies. Bernard told me:

We were booked to play nine holes of golf at the Mount Irvine Bay Hotel with Jimmy and Bruce. They were more experienced than us and since we were very new to golf, they drove off first. I hit my usual five-wood and then Tim hit an absolute screamer, which went on for miles down the fairway. Bruce was flabbergasted. 'What's that you hit, Tim?' 'A three-iron.' 'Well, you hooded the face ... You turned and ...' 'For God's sake Bruce, don't tell me what I did!'

The list of other charities with which his name was linked is endless; here is a selection, the mere tip of the iceberg: Golf Foundation, Goaldiggers, Sports Aid Foundation, Torch Trophy Trust, Riding for the Disabled, SCOPE, Duke of Edinburgh's Award Scheme (for which he gave out the certificates, played golf and attended countless fundraising dinners), National Youth Theatre, Barnardo's, Association of Boys' Clubs, NABS, Saints and Sinners, Stable Lads' Association (he and John, Lord Oaksey were trustees), Bobby Moore Fund, CLIC Sargent, the enigmatically named Guild of the XIX Lubricators (for whom he was honorary auctioneer), and latterly president of Corinthian Casuals FC.

I came across a slip of paper on which Jimmy had written the following, which sums up his willingness to help everyone and everything:

As if I hadn't enough to fill my days, I was invited to become a member of the Sports Council, under Chairman Roger Bannister. Since Sir Walter Winterbottom was its professional director, I wanted to accept. In addition, having a foot in that camp would not be a disadvantage professionally, and at the same time would enable me to play be it even a small part in improving the nation's sporting performances.

He was obviously able to fulfil his ambitions, as is evident from this letter (October 1977) from Sir Walter Winterbottom:

I have not personally expressed my thanks to you for all your valuable services in support of the Sports Council. I know my staff and colleagues deeply appreciate the way you have set about fighting for the Sports Council image and making the public aware that the Sports Council is playing an important part in the development of Sport for All.

Jimmy's admiration for Walter was boundless. In an article for the *Observer* dated January 1994, he wrote:

There are two fundamental reasons why we have lagged behind the world in mastery of the football. First, it took ages for the false belief that footballers were born and not made to die, the main executioner being Sir Walter Winterbottom.

Walter passed away in February 2002, just before his 90th birthday. Jimmy was upset by his obituary published in the *Daily Telegraph* and leapt to the defence of his old friend and mentor:

Sir Walter Winterbottom, charming man that he was, would already have forgiven the compiler of your somewhat misleading obituary. To suggest that Walter could not 'communicate' let alone inspire professional players, is nonsense. If there were those who could not understand his theories, they were in a measly minority. If some superstars initially made fun of his educated approach, they soon began to appreciate what he had to offer. During the 1950s Walter was well ahead of his time. The fact that Stanley Matthews, Tom Finney, Bobby Charlton and Jimmy Greaves were under him and an ignorant, unqualified selection committee above him, illustrated just how far collectively we had fallen behind more sophisticated countries. Nearly everyone then believed that good players were born and not made. In the latter part of the 1950s into the 1960s, a more up-to-date attitude to fitness, skill coaching and tactics became fashionable in the professional game. Walter's England, still unappreciated by some, slowly narrowed the professional gap by continuing to lead those who controlled the professional game at Lancaster Gate out of their power-struck wilderness. Ron Greenwood, Bill Nicholson, Don Revie – even Brian Clough

– made their own successful way with their own personalities and ambition, but all learnt something from Walter.

9

Jockeying for Position

The field of play is marked with lines. These lines belong to the areas of which they are boundaries.
        —*The Laws of the Game.* Law 1 - Field markings

In spite of my secretarial shortcomings, I enjoyed working in such an exciting environment, never knowing who might turn up on the doorstep from one day to the next. Within a short space of time Jimmy had become a very important part of my life and often included me in the various dos, where it was the norm to rub shoulders with leading names from the world of sport and entertainment.

In 1975, the year before we met, at the age of 47 he became unpaid managing director of Coventry City FC and was dubbed 'The Sky Blue Messiah'. Ken Widdows, in the *Coventry Evening Telegraph* on 18 April 1975, wrote:

During that time City blazed a trail of 'firsts':

1. They were the first club to introduce an answering system for fans, called *Sky Blue Rose.*
2. They were the first club with closed circuit screening when they relayed their match at Cardiff back to Highfield Road [Coventry's ground].
3. They were the first club to introduce Saturday evening soccer.
4. They were the first club to organise their own train 'specials' [the *Sky Blue Express*] for fans for away games.

Jimmy's brain was constantly on the alert to create ways and means of attracting and securing fans for the club - home and away. It has always been an ongoing battle to get the fans to travel to away matches, partly due to the costs involved, but also it is a tough call to rally support when the team isn't producing results on the field and, as Jimmy Sirrell (Notts County manager, 1983) said, 'If ye dinnae score, ye dinnae win.' The *Sky Blue Express* was a stroke of pure genius.

The flamboyant entertainer came to the fore when he rode around the ground at Highfield Road on his hunter whipping up support from the crowd, with chairman Derrick Robins following behind in his open-topped Rolls-Royce – two kinds of serious, heavy-duty horse power.

Another snippet for those history nuts among you: Coventry City used to share the nickname 'the Bantams' with Bradford City, Coventry's kit varying in colour from royal blue, jockey-style chequered green and red, or pink and navy. In 1962, Jimmy had a further light-bulb moment when he re-christened the team the Sky Blues, at the same time coming up with a revolutionary matching cerulean strip, reflecting the club's new soubriquet.

Jimmy told Neville Foulger (*Football Post and News*, 8 February 1964): 'I am not naïve enough to think that gimmicks can attract bigger crowds. Only good playing results will pull in spectators.' He also said, 'A gimmick is something which somebody wishes they had thought of first.'

It was a long, hard haul but they got to the Premiership – and stayed; only Liverpool, Arsenal and Everton could boast longer tenures.

One Sunday, while he was still unpaid managing director of the football club, Jimmy asked me if I wanted to go with him to Coventry, where the stable lads were holding a five-a-side competition following their AGM at the Ryton training ground.

In June 1975 the lads were in dispute with their bosses, the trainers, over pay and went on strike, which was resolved a month later in July. At the time about 50% in the Newmarket area were paid-up members of the Transport and General Workers' Union (TGWU). It was very different in other parts of the country where none subscribed.

Jonathan Powell (*People Sport*) wrote:

On Thursday he [Jimmy] met a number of them [the stable lads] at Lambourn in Berkshire. Hill is keen to help their cause and has asked Lord Oaksey and retired jockey Richard Pitman to help him in building up an association. The lads remember Hill as the man who, by forceful negotiation, smashed the footballers' maximum wage.

Jimmy suggested, having broken away from the TGWU, that they should call themselves the Stable Lads' Association in the same way that he had changed the name of the Players' Union to the Professional Footballers' Association.

Meetings were held in Transport House and, on arrival, Jimmy and John Oaksey were always greeted with the words, 'Good morning Lord Oaksey, Mr Hill. Trainers to the left, please,' upon which, they turned right to join the lads, much to the amusement of those behind the desk.

In searching through the box of past speech notes I came across a menu, on the back of which Jimmy had written the following:

I played a part in forming the SLA, which in a short time, along with its negotiating partners the TGWU, has transformed the wage structure and working conditions of many lads. Bad trainers = bad lads. Good trainers = good lads, who are getting something like the financial reward their highly skilled work merits. The membership now is approaching the 1000 mark, thanks to the efforts of Tommy Delaney. All young men with basic ability have the opportunity to prove themselves. I trust all in this room will think that is a worthwhile objective.

One of my tasks was to collect and bank the subs, and Jimmy thought it might be a good idea to meet some of the lads face to face, adding that I could bring Ulla (my cocker spaniel I had brought back from when I lived in France) with me. I turned up bright and early on the Sunday morning in question and found my boss in the kitchen smartly dressed in a pale butter yellow polo-neck sweater, tweed sports jacket with leather patches on the elbows and cavalry twill trousers, filling a large vacuum flask with coffee.

The day went well, apart from Ulla running onto the pitch. I continued to be invited to charity events, many of which were for the Goaldiggers, a football-orientated charity whose aim was to raise money to provide hard-surfaced playing areas. Sir Elton John was on the council, as was Jimmy of course, as well as Sir Michael Parkinson, Willis Hall (playwright and author of *The Long and the Short and the Tall*) and Brian Mears (then the chairman of Chelsea FC); Eric Morecambe was linesman and Prince Philip team coach.

On a piece of headed paper from the North London offices of Elton's agent John Reid were notes taken by Jimmy at a meeting in connection with the ball to be held at the Dorchester Hotel in May 1977. The first topic for discussion was the evening's entertainment, and Jimmy had scribbled: 'Music: Ray McVay and [the] Harry Stoneham [Trio]. Singing: Elton.'

Aimed at keeping costs to a minimum, the suggestions for the menu were: 'Mixed crudités, nibbles, assorted smoked fish followed by bangers and mash and grilled tomatoes, apple strudel and coffee.'

Unlikely fare for a five-star hotel such as the Dorchester, but Eric Morecambe said it was the first dinner at such an occasion that he had enjoyed from start to finish, eaten everything, and been tempted to lick his plate. The menu proved such a success that, at the next ball, they stuck to the same formula and served boiled beef and carrots followed by apple crumble and custard.

Elton captained his own XI in a football match against the Alan Mullery XI (Alan was then manager of Brighton and Hove Albion), and a year later, in November 1978, he persuaded Bill Oddie (a Goodie and twitcher), Billy Connolly (actor and comedian, married to Pamela Stephenson) and Dennis Waterman (actor: *Minder*, *The Sweeney* and latterly *New Tricks*) to play on his team at the Pop Five-a-Side tournament at Wembley.

Blasts from the past, members of the Hollies, Gonzalez, the Rubettes All Stars, ELO, the Stranglers, Capital Radio, Child, Darts and a motley crew who called themselves The Geriatric Rowdies comprising Jess Conrad (actor and singer with the 'ping!' smile), Robert Plant (singer/songwriter with Led Zeppelin), Jasper Carrott (actor and comedian), Dave Dee (singer/songwriter with the pop/rock group Dave Dee, Dozy, Beaky, Mick & Tich) and 'Big' Ron Atkinson (aka Mr

Bojangles, ex-manager of Manchester United and football pundit) participated, each team having its own professional sportsman.

The pulchritudinous Penthouse Pets and equally delectable Playboy Bunnies played their own five-a-side competition, thus providing plenty of bouncing half-time entertainment. What happy days they were, long before the phrase 'political correctness' had been invented, when good, clean fun was acceptable fun.

I don't think anyone realises that the majority of those celebrities who take part in hundreds of events throughout the year do so mostly at their own personal cost. To my knowledge, apart from perhaps the very odd occasion where he was given something towards petrol (which was then put back into the pot to purchase raffle tickets), Jimmy never took a halfpenny in expenses. Even during the years he was managing director and chairman at Coventry FC, director and chairman for a brief period at Charlton and chairman of Fulham, everything came out of his own pocket – for the love of the game.

10

Many a Slip 'twixt Fizz and Lip

In the summer of 1977 Jimmy decided to put the house in Bayswater on the market in order to move to the Cotswolds, thus rendering me surplus to requirements. Out of work again, salvation came from Barry Aylett, the estate agent who sold the property. His negotiator was about to get married and was going to live in Canada, and Barry, needing a replacement, asked me to work for his firm Pettigrew and Partners in Westbourne Grove, situated between a sandwich bar and an off-licence, opposite the cinema and the Baba Belphuri vegetarian Indian restaurant.

Julia Röbin (another friend from schooldays) worked at the BBC with on *Match of the Day* and suggested we meet for lunch at the canteen, where I happened to mention that I hadn't heard from Jimmy or Veronica since they moved. A few days later, I received a phone call asking if I might be free to meet Jimmy the following Saturday at the Kensington Hilton. On my arrival the concierge paged his room, then other parts of the hotel, and drew a blank.

Thinking I had confused the time and date I made my way to the exit, only to see his familiar figure emerge from the bar, dressed in jeans and a sweatshirt, looking tanned and fit. Visibly relieved, he greeted me warmly, and said he had been on his way to phone home to find out if something had happened. His eyes sparkled even more than usual, possibly due to the champagne he had been sharing with Dougie Hayward (Fulham fan, Arsenal supporter and tailor to the stars whose list of clients included Clint Eastwood, Steve McQueen, Michael Caine, Terence Stamp and Mick Jagger.)

There was still time for a speedy bite before Jimmy had to whizz off to the studios. 'Sorry it's been a bit of a mix-up,' Jimmy said. 'Let me make it up to you and have supper before the programme.'

The Balzac on Shepherd's Bush Green was small and intimate, the tables set with open parasols as though outside on a terrace on the French Riviera. The bill paid, Jimmy asked if I wanted to watch the programme only a minute away in Wood Lane. I had never been on a television set before; everywhere was a confused mass of fat cables, wires and lights, and when the final credits rolled Jimmy unplugged his earpiece and beckoned me over. 'Don't let's end it here,' he said, as we slipped on our coats.

He drove me to the Saddle Room in Park Lane (London's first disco, now closed), ordered a bottle of champagne and asked me to dance. And then he kissed me.

Lordy, lordy. What on earth could I have been thinking? But there was no getting away from it: here I was, suddenly on very friendly terms with my old boss, a man twenty-three years older than me and with a very complicated private life. We returned to our table, my heart thumping a military tattoo, not knowing where to look or what to say.

We left the club, stopping on the way for me to pick up my Mini. In my rear-view mirror I noticed Jimmy didn't turn north to Bayswater but was following me back to Hammersmith.

'Oh, what a tangled web we weave when first we practise to deceive.'

In spite of protestations on my part Jimmy stayed the night, leaving at first light to rush off to Heathrow in order to catch his monthly flight to Saudi. Punching well above my weight and convinced I would never hear from him again, later that week I received a postcard written on the plane as it began its descent into Heathrow:

Friday. Darling Bun – just landing at London Airport after a very relaxing visit. Oodles of sleep, some sunshine, no work, but sadly no you either. Thank you for everything – we'll dream together.

The postcard came as a complete shock, and then the telephone calls started. I was enjoying working at Pettigrews and Jimmy soon became a frequent visitor, and, if I had time, took me out for a leisurely lunch. One balmy summer's evening a few weeks later when he was away in the States, Chris Lewis, floor manager at BBC Sport, asked me out for a drink.

I parked my car in an alleyway in Wimbledon Village and walked over to the Dog and Fox pub, where I found Chris propping up the bar with none other than John Thaw and Dennis Waterman. John was currently playing Detective Jack Regan in the hugely popular police drama *The Sweeney*, and Dennis, his sidekick DS George Carter. I was showered in flattery (undeserved) and fizz (definitely deserved) and had a perfectly lovely time. The offer of going out to dinner with my new best friends was tempting but I declined: Jimmy was due to ring me and I wanted to hear his voice.

That December, after a reception for the Guild of the XIX Lubricators in the Lord Speaker's Room at the House of Commons, Jimmy skedaddled to the all-male Christmas lunch, leaving me to my own devices. As I strolled past the gates of the Parliament buildings, who should be on duty but dear old Gordon, our friendly policeman who used to patrol the streets near Pettigrews in Notting Hill. Recognising me, he came over and gave me a big kiss on the cheek – just as Jimmy sped past in a taxi to the Stafford Hotel. 'Miss B!' he shouted through the window, 'I can't leave you alone for a second!'

11

Spiritual Intervention

Jimmy ended an article for his old school magazine with these following thoughts:

> To some people soccer is more than a game to be played and enjoyed, irrespective of colour, crowd appeal, number a side, play-ground or field, or even player status. They use soccer as a means of up-holding the great tradition of games snobbery, against the weight of opinion in our changing society. It is tragic that so often the real spirit of soccer has to be saved from its well-meaning but misguided administrators and I am afraid sometimes from its equally misguided younger players. Still there have been changes for the better and there will be more, I hope.

A few years later, in the introduction to his regular column for the match day programme during his time at Coventry City FC, he wrote:

> I don't pretend to be a fortune teller and certainly not a gipsy, but I am prepared to try my hand and predict the way football will progress in the Eighties. There are three ways to look ahead. The first, to imagine things that almost certainly will happen; then to imagine things that might well happen and, perhaps the most enjoyable of all, although it can lead to a fair amount of frustration, to wish for all things that one would like to see happen. We must never forget the spirit of football, which for me is exemplified, not so much by world stars winning world cup competitions nor yet legendary players stirring our memories. It's more of the pleasure that a young boy gets of

rushing out onto the nearest piece of grass with a new pair of boots, or a new ball on Christmas morning. The fun he gets is the fun we should all continue to see from this extraordinarily satisfying game.

Annie, my colleague at Pettigrews, was intrigued by the paranormal and just before we packed up for Christmas booked a consultation at the headquarters of the Spiritualist Association of Great Britain in Belgrave Square, and suggested that I go with her.

We walked into the impressive building and, while Annie was ushered into one room, I was directed to another. I had no idea what I was letting myself in for. On entering a darkened study, a table lamp providing the only illumination, I saw a 'mumsy' grey-haired woman seated behind a desk. She peered over the top of her glasses. 'Come and sit down. You haven't come in alone, my dear. Don't be frightened. He's not of the afterlife, although he is much older than you. In fact he is very much with you, standing right behind you, at your left shoulder. He will never leave your side.'

Part Two
The Eighties – A Busy Decade

12

Bratby, Booze and Blunders

In March 1980, I took the day off work to accompany Jimmy to Hastings to have his portrait painted by the 'kitchen-sink realist' artist John Bratby (1928-92). He was doing a series of portraits of famous people in the world of politics, theatre and music that he called 'A Gallery of Individuals', and this was the reason behind his approach to Jimmy. Amongst other sitters were Michael Foot (who used the same National Health dentist as us in Camden – now there's a claim to fame), Paul McCartney, Cyril Smith, the actress Billie Whitelaw and the author Lady Antonia Fraser.

We drove down to the south coast in Jimmy's newly acquired gold (it was the Eighties), wedge-shaped Lotus Elite. Mr Bratby's wife Patti welcomed us, swiftly followed by her husband, who appeared from the kitchen. 'Come into the studio, James,' he said. 'Patti will make you a bacon sandwich and a cup of tea.' He nodded in my direction. 'Perhaps your friend could go shopping?'

When I returned four hours later it was still daylight and, since Jimmy always travelled with his golf clubs, he wanted to see if he could fit in a few holes at Rye, a private members' club on the links at Camber Sands – a wish he had long harboured. Whenever such an opportunity arose, rather than expecting to be granted courtesy of the course he always liked to ask first if there was any chance of hitting a few balls. He located the secretary, who handed Jimmy the membership list.

'Have a look and see if there is a name you recognise, Mr Hill.'

'Here's someone,' he confirmed, 'Sandy Gall [journalist, writer and ITN news reporter].'

'Perfect. Then I shall put you down as his guest, but you should be aware the bar closes on the dot of seven.'

Darkness was falling fast and we only managed to play the first nine and then cut across the dunes towards the clubhouse. As Jimmy was tucking the clubs in the boot a shout came from across the car park. It was the steward. 'Mr Hill,' he said, 'There's plenty of time. Come in and have a drink before you go. The secretary might think he runs the place but everyone knows I do!'

The bar (in those days - possibly even today) was 100% male territory; even Margaret Thatcher wasn't allowed into the holy of holies when accompanying her husband Dennis - but on that particular evening I was an exception to the rule. Our kindly host must have made some telephone calls, because gradually one or two members drifted in. It turned into quite a party and, having consumed one too many, I disgraced myself and fell off my stool.

Several weeks later, in May, Jimmy was surprised to receive a letter from John Bratby with an unexpected request:

Send me a cheque for £350. I enclose a SAE to save you time. I take it that you want me to keep it [the picture] in my studio for you. But would you like me to send it to the framer? Remember that any time you give me a call I can get it delivered to your home. To turn to less mundane considerations I did see the England v Argentina match and enjoyed it very much. I shall certainly watch very carefully in the press for developments of your anti-hooliganism campaign but 1981/82 seems a long way away and a lot of damage can be done in the meantime. With regard to my portraits about 'Individuality' (perhaps our letters crossed for I mentioned Hans Keller to you) I am thinking about initially dividing into areas of activity and to have an exhibition of people of Music and Dance at the Royal Festival Hall, and so on. I would like to have a separate exhibition of people of sport. Yourself, John Conteh, Lord Hunt, Sir Alec Rose, Chay Blyth, Clare Francis, Colin Cowdrey - all of whom I have painted. I would like an appropriate exhibition area where sportsmen see pictures of sportsmen. Does an idea occur to you on this? If there is any way I can help with the hooliganism problem, let me know, as I feel about it as deeply as you.

Hans Keller, an Austrian-born musician, among other activities, coached at the Menuhin School of Music until his death. His controversial comments in a debate with Pink Floyd, whilst puffing on a cigarette, were recorded in May 1967 for the BBC Radio programme *Look of the Week* and can be viewed online.

John wrote in a further letter to Jimmy: 'This is just to tell you that Hans Keller in his book *1984 minus 9* [1975] has written an ultimate chapter on the decline of football and the decline of individualism in it.'

Bratby's portrait of Jimmy can be seen in the National Football Museum in Preston for all to enjoy. However, due to recent revelations in connection with Sir Cyril Smith's private life, John Bercow, Commons Speaker, had Smith's portrait by the artist removed from the Palace of Westminster.

Jimmy's main sporting contribution for charity, apart from the odd tennis or cricket match, was golf. When he was asked to take part in a competition on the Isle of Man, he said that if I was able to take time off work, I could go too. I was earning very little; my one and only black dress had to see me through the two nights and I prayed that, by ringing the changes with different jackets, no one would notice.

The first evening we attended a cocktail party at Robert Sangster's impressive house, the Nunnery. Robert was an incredibly successful racehorse owner and breeder, and *le tout société* of the island was present. Jimmy was snaffled instantly by ex-England cricketer Colin Ingleby-Mackenzie and Charles 'the Scout' Benson, racing correspondent for the *Daily Express*. Abandoned and feeling like a drab fowl in my dull plumage, I hugged the skirting boards and must have looked a pretty pathetic lump standing on my own. Help came when a smiling man carrying a tray of flutes filled with champagne wended his way purposefully across the room towards me. 'You look a little lost,' he said. 'Here, take one of these – it's the good stuff – but keep it to yourself!' After I had quaffed a couple of glasses matters improved and a small group of us – including Colin and Charles – went out to dinner, where I discovered my knight in shining armour was none other than Robert Sangster himself.

We were staying in a hotel on the esplanade in the capital Douglas and, having explored the island the day before and knowing there would be spectacular sea views, I decided to gain a few 'Bryony' points by pulling Jimmy's trolley. The sun shone brightly and, as we were waiting for his tee-off time, a local chap called George Hotchkiss (who was employed at the local hospital) offered to relieve me of the duty. A mine of useful information, he was an excellent caddy and for several years sent us boxes of Manx kippers carefully wrapped in polystyrene boxes recycled from work. I dread to think what they had previously contained.

Rick Wakeman (musician, songwriter and keyboard player for the rock band Yes) had brought his wife Nina Carter with him. In the Seventies Nina and her stablemate Jilly Johnson became household names, famous as glamour models posing on page three of the *Sun* newspaper. We were an unlikely pairing – I am certainly not a rock chick, chicky, chicky rock chick, more a case of rock cake, rocky, rocky rock cake – but we hit it off and, rather than tag along with Rick, she kept me company.

From 1980–81, *Match of the Day* was moved from late Saturday night to the more family-friendly slot on Sunday afternoons. Jimmy went to the studio in the morning to prepare the script and then returned to Notting Hill for grilled bacon, tomatoes, toast and large mugs of tea followed by the ritual of bathing and hair washing. Once the final credits ran he would rush back in time to catch *The Muppet Show*. Saturday nights were suddenly free – a novelty – and we often went out for a meal.

On one particular evening Jimmy dropped me off outside our favourite Chinese restaurant in Queensway to bag a table while he parked the car and went to get the early editions of the Sunday papers. It was a busy night and the ground floor was full, so I was shown to the downstairs dining room. I asked for some jasmine tea. Ten minutes went by; a couple sat at the table next to me and ordered their meal. After thirty minutes, still with no sign of Jimmy, I was very worried indeed. The couple paid the bill and left. I looked at my watch. By then I had been sitting on my own for over an hour. I grabbed a passing waiter.

'This *is* the New Lee Ho Fook, isn't it?'

'No. This Hung Tao. New Lee Ho Fook next door.'

Oh fook.

13

Light-bulb Moments

Jimmy never gave up on a dream. In the Eighties hooliganism and football seemed indelibly linked. He was constantly being told that rugby and cricket didn't suffer in the same way. Why? Jimmy would reply that, whenever there had been a lengthy period without a major war, problems arose at home, and football took the blame – adding that it wasn't football's problem but the fault of society. Egged on by his desire to beat the thugs at their own game, Jimmy managed to get the go-ahead to construct an all-seater stadium at Coventry City's Highfield Road ground (Jimmy: 'You can't be a hooligan sitting down'), the first of its kind in the English football league. Revolutionary in design, there would be no crush barriers; no barricades; no fences of any sort and no 'cattle pens'.

In an interview with Ken Widdows (*Coventry Evening Telegraph*, 14 April 1981) Jimmy said:

> There should be no violence and no bad language. The beauty about having such a ground is that all seats are numbered, and any offenders can be identified. They will not be allowed to return to Highfield Road. We want to make it a happy place for every decent family, where they can watch soccer in peace and contentment.

His wish had come true, and a few months later, Coventry were at home to Leeds United. With Leeds losing four goals to nil, a riot erupted when the frustrated visiting fans starting ripping out hundreds of the seats, causing the game to be abandoned. A well-known building society had the slogan, 'Say the Leeds and you're smiling.' Not on that day they weren't.

A considerable debate was developing concerning the merits of recorded football highlights on television versus the transmission of live games. In November 1981 Brian Moore (Jimmy's counterpart at ITV) wrote to him with the following suggestions prior to a Group 6 meeting of the Football League:

Recorded football no longer captures big audiences. Neither *MOTD* nor ITV's Sunday afternoon football has ever been in the top 20. *Parkinson* is now promoted ahead of *MOTD*, which has lost every week in the ratings against ITV's Saturday night film. Live football still commands a big audience. But selected live matches through the season in mid-week could not generate the same sort of finance as the present recorded system does. The Television Companies would insist on only major First Division games being screened – with respect to them, there is no point in putting on Gillingham [Brian had been a director of Gillingham FC for 7 years] v Doncaster at peak time: there would be a huge downturn in ground advertising.

Jimmy always said that if he took a penny for every pound he had raised on the rostrum he would be richer than Croesus. I have never seen anyone steer an auction better – even those tried-and-trusted professionals for whom it is their day job. Jimmy's secret was to prepare thoroughly beforehand, noting the value of the items and calculating the increments he would use between bids, and then inveigling the captive audience to lift their hands with hushed persuasion. The punters lapped it up. Generous to a fault, should a lot not attract the buyers he would make a bid. Undoubtedly the most successful auctions he undertook were for NABS (the National Advertisers' Benevolent Fund) at its annual boxing evening. It was always a rowdy stag affair, and for nearly a quarter of a century, each successive year he beat his previous record in terms of the total amount raised. At the dinner on 7 November 1983 at the Royal Lancaster Hotel in London, after skilful haranguing, he managed to extract £97,000, a phenomenal sum in those days. A representative of Gillette approached Jimmy in the boxing ring and said that if they fetched one of their razors and he shaved off his beard, they would cough up an extra £3,000 to round it up to £100,000.

I'll return to this story in a moment, but on the subject of Jimmy's beard, George Cohen told me the following anecdote from when he and Jimmy were at Fulham together:

My outstanding memory of Jimmy was in the Sixties and heavily involved with the PFA in negotiating wage rises in footballers' salaries. It was also the time when he decided to grow a goatee beard. He was, without a doubt, very enthusiastic playing in midfield and supporting the great Johnny Haynes. In one particular game [at Fulham], after making several runs into space calling for the ball and not getting it, he became somewhat frustrated and started to demand more of the ball in no uncertain terms. The crowd thought it was hilarious. He made a cross run in front of me [George was playing right-back] and he made it very clear in a very high voice, that he wanted the ball played to him. This brought a response from one cockney supporter who yelled, 'For Christ's sake Cohen, give the ball to the Rabbi.' Obviously, Jimmy's beard and my Jewish name brought a roar of approval from the fans. While I don't remember the result of the match, I do remember how seriously Jimmy took our national game.

Jimmy continued to keep up with George, and played in his benefit match at Fulham on 10 November 1969. Jimmy wrote:

I remember only too well the day, as an ex-Fulham player, I returned to Craven Cottage to play with some of my middle-aged colleagues for the George Cohen testimonial fund.

The old boys, giving away something like ten to fifteen years a man, began to perform surprisingly well and, to their own astonishment, as well as that of the crowd, took the lead. The Fulham lads began to get rather edgy realising that the boys of the old brigade were not going to relinquish one goal advantage without a fight.

Suddenly, Bobby Robson broke through on the right of the

goal, and shot fiercely against the goalkeeper's feet. The ball spun wickedly in the air in my direction – at an angle – about 15 yards from goal. I knew that I had to volley it – only a coward would have shirked that responsibility – and there was no way I wanted to be accused of that. So, doing my best to ignore the fact that the chances of me hitting the goal must have been around 20-1, I closed my eyes and lashed at the ball. To my complete astonishment, it flew into the back of the net without the goalkeeper moving an inch. I had never volleyed a ball more sweetly in the 12 years of my professional career. Once the crowd had recovered its composure, a long suffering supporter was heard to remark, 'It's a pity they didn't bloody well play like that when they were here!'

Returning to the NABS evening, the BBC was currently on strike and Jimmy reckoned he would have time to grow back his beard before he was on air again. Without hesitation he said, 'I'll do it.' When I heard his key rattle in the door it was well past 3.00 a.m.

'How did you get on?' I asked.

'We beat last year and topped a hundred grand!'

'Wow!' I said, kicking off the duvet and getting out of bed. 'I'll make us some Ovaltine.'

Jimmy looked at me strangely. 'Haven't you noticed?'

'Eh?'

He pointed to his chin: the beard had gone.

Bruce Forsyth said it was because we were still 'at the looking-in-the-eyes' stage.

14

He Fought the Law and the Law Won

A player shall be cautioned if:
  - he persistently infringes the Laws of the Game, or
  - he persists in misconduct after having received a caution.
          —The Laws of the Game. Law 12 – Fouls and Misconduct

A piece of music entitled *Devil's Galop* by Charles Williams was used as the signature tune for the BBC Light Programme wireless play *Dick Barton – Special Agent*, broadcast from 1946 to 1951. Those of you mature enough to remember it, hum it as you read the next few paragraphs.

Jimmy never took a test because they were suspended during the war, only having become compulsory a few years previously, in 1935. In a magazine article, he wrote:

It was a wonder I ever survived those early motoring experiences. At sixteen I bought a 250cc BSA motor bike with no kick start – in the war with no spare parts it was a run-and-jump-on job. A move to a 1930 Austin Seven saloon was heaven until going down the hill into Folkestone with a full two boy-two girlfriend load, I ran out of road on a bend and we all ended up in Folkestone Hospital.

When Jimmy played for Fulham in the Fifties they used to go down to the south coast to Worthing for summer training, booking in at the prestigious Warnes Hotel situated on the seafront. The morning's work over, there would be a mad dash to get back to HQ in order to be first out of the traps to bag the limited amount of hot water for a much-needed bath. George Cohen, whose entire professional career was with the Thames-side club and who was in the victorious 1966 World Cup team, told me that Jimmy would be at the wheel of his car before anybody else. One day (long before the wearing of seat belts was law) Jimmy gave George a lift and a bit of a race sparked between them and another teammate. Unfortunately, the road was too narrow to accommodate two vehicles side by side and, with no room to overtake, Jimmy mounted the pavement and manoeuvred his car into pole position. George said he had never been so frightened – even when facing the German defence.

In the late Seventies *Sportswide* included a 'Mini Stox' race with kids, and they asked Jimmy to have a go. Completely disregarding the fact that he was old enough to be their grandfather, and subjected to persistent ramming by the pubescent boys, he cottoned on that the weak did not win. He came a respectable third, the bruises he had received in the battering a badge of honour.

There were unfortunately other occasions when he put his foot to the metal a touch too fiercely, but on Her Majesty's highway.

A letter arrived from the Chief Constable of Warwickshire Police, Roger Birch:

I had a message this morning from Chief Superintendent Fretwell to say that, reluctantly, he has no option but to pursue your speeding offence in the normal way through the Courts. Many years in this game has taught me that the only way I can live with myself as a policeman is to treat everyone the same and, as I mentioned to you on the telephone, I have a fair number of friends who 'con' me for a gin and tonic every time I see them on the strength of their appearance in Court for various misdemeanours – mostly speeding! I am sure that if you were in my position, knowing your concern for fair play, you would think precisely the same and I think I know you well enough already to know that you will not hold it against us for making this decision. We will do our best to make it up to you on the evening when you have kindly agreed to help us out with our Crime Prevention Quiz and I am sure this is all the more reason why it would be prudent for me to provide you with transport as promised!!

15

Portrait of a Twentieth-century Crusader

At a seminar in October 1980, Jimmy presented a paper to the Football League; some of the topics to be discussed were:

Structure of the League and how to make the League Competition more attractive including, 'Facilities and hassle, miserable and aggressive atmosphere: bad publicity – paid for, bad publicity – provided free, and it looks as if clubs don't care.'

Under the heading 'Suggested Amendments to the Points System', Jimmy had written in the margin: 'Away win – three points', an idea he put forward to encourage more attacking play.

In a memorandum headed 'Isthmian League Sponsorship Scheme', Jimmy wrote:

Further to my original proposition it was decided after a discussion with Mr T. Williams representing Rothman's and Mr D. Insole attending on behalf of the Isthmian League and myself that, in the interest of both players and spectators, the scheme would be finalised on the lines set out in this document.

1. ATTACKING FOOTBALL
    The points system in both Divisions of the League to be changed, so that three points are given for a win and only one for a draw.
2. GOAL INCENTIVES
    Weekly awards
    If a club wins a match by three clear goals it will be paid a bonus of £40 in the First Division and £35 in the Second.

Season's awards
These awards will apply to clubs who have not received a cash prize for finishing first, second or third in their respective divisions and will be as follows:
Highest scorers Division I – £300, 2nd highest scorers – £200, 3rd highest scorers – £100
Division 2 – £150, £100 and £50.

Those amounts seem laughable and would hardly cover the cost of a meal for two these days – without wine.

This new law of Three Points for a Win was introduced in England a year later in 1981 and then adopted worldwide. The headlines in the *Evening Standard* on 27 October 1980 for an article by Peter Blackman read:

Soccer to wage war over TV
The explosive issue of television soccer coverage and payment was sure to provoke an angry debate among the Football League's 92 club chairman today. That assurance came from Fulham's prickly chief Ernie Clay who told me, 'The cameras are wrecking our game because of over-exposure.'

The article continued to report the proposals put forward in Solihull:

Freedom to play matches on Sunday
The season starting in September and ending in May
Fifteen minute half time break to promote more crowd entertainment and,
Changes in how transfer fees are paid.

Following the seminar Mr Clay wrote to Jimmy:

Now that the great Meeting or Seminar is over, I must tell you this, as the World's greatest stirrer. I did not give two shillings for its survival during the first twenty minutes hence my little 'act', and I must congratulate you, Stephen [Kew, Chairman of Bristol City FC] and Graham [Kelly, Secretary of the Football

League], for steering it over that very delicate time. I have a very old saying – before you can 'nick' the gold out of Fort Knox you have to get the door open and, by golly, you three opened the door. I am sending you some of the wine crushed with my own feet – but I can assure you, not before I washed them.

The meeting prompted a letter from Stephen Kew, who wrote on 28 October:

What a great success the last two days were! There is no need to form a mutual admiration society, but I am sure you know what I mean when I express my thanks for your help especially where I was concerned. Perhaps you could give me a ring soon – you can reverse the charges if you wish!

The impact on world football of this change in the law was un-imaginable. In July 1994 a Mr Rex Van Rossum sent a letter addressed to '*World Cup Grandstand*':

About 20 years ago Jimmy Hill walked into my office with a proposal to sponsor non-League football. I was then the Marketing Director of Rothman's and, since we already sponsored almost everything else that moved, I was not enthusiastic ahead of the meeting. But with great panache Jimmy laid before me a set of highly imaginative new ideas to encourage sportsmanship and attacking football – including 3 points for a win. Like Victor Kiam, 'I was so impressed I bought the Company' [the company being Remington. Victor Kiam became internationally famous when he starred in an advertisement for their revolutionary razor]. So we did it – and it was a great success. In the very first season more non-League clubs reached the 3rd and 4th rounds of the FA Cup than in 'living memory'. Then the Football League adopted it ... Now the World Cup ... both with great success.

A few months later in October that year, Mr Van Rossum wrote a personal letter to Jimmy:

81

I was delighted to see Michael Herd's piece in the *Evening Standard* of last week placing you as No 9 (centre-forward!) in his all-time list of good influences on British sport. Not only that, he gives you the accolade based on your work re abolition of the minimum [*sic* –a slip many people make] wage and as the pioneer of 3 points for a win. So you see, there is some justice after all. Creativity will out.

The controversy surrounding the change in the law continued. In May 1996 Richard Colbey (a barrister and freelance football writer) wrote an article in the *Daily Telegraph*:

I'm a Watford fan, and only one First Division team has drawn more games this season. Because 15 years ago the Football League decreed that wins were to be worth three points against one for a draw. Watford spent much of the season looking like certainties for relegation. This system was introduced in the belief that it would lead to attacking football. Ironic isn't it then that a team who have scored 62 goals should be relegated because of this quirk of having drawn so many games?

Jimmy replied to the newspaper:

I read with interest Barrister Richard Colbey's loss of affection for the system. What he failed to appreciate in regurgitating the immediate slow, statistical effect of the change was that, as result of negative tactics stagnation had already stubbornly set in. It was designed to encourage attack, but even more to prevent teams shutting up shop in negative fashion long before the game's end, having captured 50% of the afternoon's cake. In claiming game, set and match for a legally unqualified but experienced old pro', may I destroy Mr Colbey's reasoning totally by referring to his last sentence: 'It would make sense to differentiate between goalless games and scoring draws.' Quite simply and irrevocably, it cannot be allowed for opposing teams to gain by a common course of action, i.e. we'll score a goal each and then begin the game in earnest. I'll concede one point

– there would never be another goalless draw. In addition to individual games, the up-and-down seesaw swings that can arise in the League table maintain interest for longer in the season, as Watford's late but unsuccessful surge proved.

Jimmy cared, perhaps more than anyone, about how the game of football was changing – not necessarily (in his opinion) for the better. A man constantly on a mission, his greatest wish would have been to see ex-professional footballers taking on the role of referee when they retired from playing. That way, he said, the game would be fairer as no one knew the tricks of the trade better than someone who had played the game at a professional level. However, thanks to the abolition of the maximum wage, with players earning small fortunes and the prospect of a financially secure retirement, what incentive is there to pursue the rigorous training programme?

16

Never a Dull Moment

A trip to the theatre or a concert was generally a spur-of-the-moment decision, and one Saturday in February 1981 Jimmy dropped into my office for a coffee and suggested we went out that evening, as it was my birthday the next day. Looking through the paper we discovered that John Ogdon was due to perform at the Royal Festival Hall on the South Bank. Larger than life and in his mid-forties, he suffered from severe bouts of depression and that day was bravely attempting a comeback. Unfortunately, due to traffic, we arrived minutes after the performance had started but were able to enjoy the opening rendition from the wings. Once in our seats we sat in complete awe (and in tears) as we listened to this gentle genius play Beethoven's Piano Concerto No. 5 in E-flat major (Emperor), Op. 73.

With the atmosphere in the concert hall electric, the last note a fading memory, John stood up. The audience erupted. In a world of his own and, I sensed, almost embarrassed by the effect his playing had produced, he shuffled from the stage. I shall never forget it and, as it happened, nor did Jimmy. In October 1998 David Mellor interviewed him on his programme *Across the Threshold* for Classic FM and Jimmy mentioned how he was deeply affected by John's presence and his playing. A week or so later a letter arrived from Brenda Ogdon, John's widow:

> I am writing to thank you for your really delightful appreciation of my late husband. It was a really lovely interview and I know that John would have been absolutely thrilled. Did you go backstage to meet John? If not, what a great shame, because John loved football and used to attend matches in Manchester in his youth. He was a passionate admirer of George Best. John's

genius was outstanding and the warmth of his personality moved everyone with whom he came into contact. The tragedy of his life and career is a national one, so programmes like yours are really widely appreciated by many people.

The merry-go-round of management never runs out of steam. In May 1981 Dave Sexton, recently sacked by Manchester United, replaced Gordon Milne at Coventry. Before the appointment, as chairman of the club, Jimmy wanted to interview Dave, but in order to foil the press, he needed to find a suitable venue, as the last thing he wanted was to have journalists lying in wait outside on the pavement. The anonymity provided by our flat in Pembridge Crescent was ideal. Before I left for work that morning I prepared a tray of cups, coffee pot and some biscuits, and when I returned in the evening I found a note from Jimmy: 'The coffee worked game, set and match! xxx'.

Bridget Köllerström (my landlady from Westcroft Square in Hammersmith) gave me some advice, which I prayed I would never have to fall back on. Bridget had been a dancer with the Royal Ballet Company at Covent Garden, and when she retired, she choreographed certain scenes both for the Opera House and for the avant-garde revue *Oh! Calcutta!* at the Duchess Theatre; from the sublime to the ridiculous.

Her late husband was Oscar Köllerström, a psychoanalyst and former pupil of Georg Groddeck, the 'father of psychosomatic medicine', and she herself was a trained psychotherapist. 'A time might come when you have to let go. It will hurt but it will be a positive move, of that I can assure you,' Bridget advised me. 'Have the courage to recognise this and be strong and whichever way the pendulum swings good will come out of it.'

Summer holidays presented a problem. While Jimmy went to Spain to spend time with his family I went to Cornwall with my mother. I was heading for 30. I wanted a husband, children and a normal life (whatever that is). I had reached that pivotal moment Bridget had predicted and, wearing my heart on my sleeve, told Jimmy (then in his early fifties) that I couldn't carry on with the uncertainty any longer.

Forced between a rock and a hard place, he was devastated but agreed that I should be free to find someone closer to my own age, which, until then, had never been an issue. I accepted invitations to dinner or the theatre. But after a brief period of silence, Jimmy found it impossible to let go, phoning me constantly and turning up at the office without warning. Late one night, as I was walking along the crescent from having been out to supper with a neighbour, I saw his car. Our love stronger than we realised, the deal was off.

To be fair, he never kidded me that he would change his mind, a point he made very clear in one of his little notes: 'Darling B, I'm allergic to weddings! I adore ecstatic weekends! Thank you my darling. I'll be back soon. Weekend Wilf alias Jim the Slim xxxx'.

Very much in love and with the bit between my teeth, on I plodded, tenacious as a Rottweiler.

'Darling girl,' he wrote, 'I'm having my own problems. It'll soon be better. Love and kisses, Aching Arthur.'

That summer, Jimmy took me to his old stamping ground, Aigua Blava on the Costa Brava in Northern Spain. This was a major step up the ladder, but one which made me extremely nervous. The regular visitors to this tiny Catalan resort had known each other for years but by treading gently, everyone was very kind and welcoming and I found it easier following in so many formidable footsteps than I had feared.

Rene and Sydney Carr – the senior vanguard – proved more difficult nuts to crack and Jimmy, realising the potential minefield, thought it a good idea to invite them to supper. Taking a bite out of a piece of bread, Rene said with amazing bluntness, 'To be perfectly honest Bryony, we didn't like you at first.' Sydney gulped his wine. His wife battled on, 'But you improve on knowing.'

When taking a plane, Jimmy would have the car picked up by a local firm who garaged it while he was away. One day he asked me to do the booking.

'Hello,' I said, 'I'm ringing on behalf of Mr Jimmy Hill.'

'Are you the Mrs 'ill what goes doggin'?'

He was, I hasten to add, referring to whippet coursing and not the, ahem, other activity.

17

'Ma'as salamah' to Saudi Arabia and *'Howdy!'* to the $tates

If you can make one heap of all your winnings
And risk it on one turn of pitch-and-toss,
And lose, and start again at your beginnings
And never breathe a word about your loss,
If you can force your heart and nerve and sinew
To serve your turn long after they are gone,
And so hold on when there is nothing in you
Except the Will which says to them,: 'Hold on!'

—from Rudyard Kipling, *If*

This period in Jimmy's professional career is complex. In 1979, following differences of opinion, Jimmy's company World Sports Academy left the Middle East when its contract was passed onto a Brazilian group.

'Happily,' he says in his autobiography, 'we parted friends'.

However, two years previously, in 1977, the WSA compass was already pointing west across the Atlantic with a view to investigating the possibility of bidding for a franchise in America. Jimmy sent Duncan to the States in order to investigate the situation there. After quite a battle, WSA was successful in defeating five other consortia in securing exclusive rights to Detroit Express in the NASL (North American Soccer League).

I quote once more from *The Jimmy Hill Story*: 'The reason WSA wanted to take on a franchise was to re-invest the money we were earning from our Saudi Arabian contract. Had we brought it back to Britain, 90% would have disappeared in tax.'

In an article by Jim Crace which appeared in the *Telegraph Sunday Magazine* in May 1982, Jimmy is quoted as saying when he invested in Detroit Express, 'They [the Americans] have a fresh approach to football. They're not hidebound. We held a trial for local players and 180 showed up, 60 of them women!'

It proved to be a larger task than he imagined because, in spite of healthy figures supplied by the NASL, the truth of the matter was very different. The Americans were used to the aggressive, fast, rough-and-tumble theatrical drama of their 'football', and our 'soccer', as the game is known in the States, was fighting an uphill struggle. It was accused of being slow and repetitive and, in particular – perhaps the biggest growl of all – of having a paucity of goals. Added to these negatives was the pressure of running the stadium with low gate receipts and the vast distances between clubs making attending away matches a costly challenge. This series of pitfalls, even with his messianic desire to get the game off the ground, was almost impossible to surmount.

Good money was poured onto bad, but while there were some successes on the field, it was essential to keep a financial head above water, with money tumbling hand over fist down the pan. A miracle suddenly shimmered on the horizon when there came the suggestion that 'a number of rich Washington businessmen' would welcome a new franchise. Jimmy wrote, 'We had a series of discussions with potential partners, and on Friday, 27 February, 1981 at precisely 2.00 p.m., the directors of the NASL unanimously approved the relocation of the franchise to Washington DC. We were heralded by the Washington media as saviours for bringing soccer back to the capital.'

Jimmy was going to stay in America all summer, and he invited me to fly over to join him for two weeks in July. 'Hello, darling girl,' he wrote, 'only 13 days to go before "B" day.' I should have known that a leopard doesn't change its spots and – in the next paragraph, he gave a full-blown report of the Washington Diplomats' current situation:

A lot has happened with regard to the team following our 6–1 losing streak. I interviewed all the players and afterwards told Ken Furphy [the manager] that we were going to attack rather than defend and if we lost, I'd take the responsibility. We were

2-1 down at half time to San Diego but fortunately came back to 2 all and won the shoot-out, so broke the sequence of four losing games in a row. It gets quite depressing with not enough money and the team losing when they play, especially when they don't score goals and earn no points at all. Johann Cruyff is now signed on and came on for the last 15 minutes of the game. The crowd went wild, but with his groin injury still not healed he's slower than me, but he did direct the other players well.

On the point of losing the will to live, I perked up:

I'm so looking forward to seeing you darling girl and it won't be long now. I miss you and send all my love and promises to my sweetheart, love JH. PS Don't buy any clothes. We'll go shopping when you get here.

Two days later I received another letter.

My darling girl, the second telecast from Montreal went even better than the first and, if I'm not careful, I'll become a celebrity! Our next away trip is to Portland and from there we fly down to the West Coast to play California. I'm considering hiring a car and driving down to take in that very special coastline. I only wish you had been able to come out earlier and we could have done it together. I went to the White House with 500 other athletes on Monday evening. We were both impressed with the President's performance [Ronald Reagan] – it was most professional, his speech being sincere – and funny, too. We didn't meet him but the vodka's very strong at the White House, I do know that! I miss you very much indeed and hope that you miss me, too, if only in making the flat look lived in! All my love, my darling, your own Wandering Wilfred. Xxxx

Jimmy had arranged for my air ticket to be sent from Washington asking the club secretary to deal with the arrangements. With only days before my scheduled departure there was still no sign of it and I began to panic. Luckily, it arrived and I understood instantly why there had been such a delay: it had been sent by surface mail.

I was put through an intensive inquisition at immigration at Dulles International Airport: Who paid for my ticket? Where was I staying? How long was I staying? Who with? Thankfully Jimmy was waiting for me at the barrier in kit I did not recognise but which he had mentioned previously in a letter: 'I've bought a cream leather jacket, trousers in three shades and a super-expensive brown silk shirt – it's irresistible to touch.'

We hit the freeway in his air-conditioned hired saloon and drove to the rented house where he was staying. Jimmy showed me round the property and, on seeing the mess everywhere, drawers open and the contents spilling onto the floor, (1) I felt instantly at home since Jimmy had once said that if there was an Olympic category for untidiness I would knock Steve Redgrave's five gold medals into a cocked hat, although (2) I wondered whether burglars had beaten us to it. 'The cleaner has been,' Jimmy said, laughing at the look on my face. 'Imagine what it was like beforehand!'

In a letter from my father dated 9 December 1964, he wrote:

Darling Bun Bun Bun, please, please make a Christmas resolution to be more tidy. Ma has been right through your bedroom and the playroom. If you take anything out PUT IT AWAY NEATLY. You have been warned. Disobey and you will be tied up in the sentry box [the old outside loo] and starved for three days and nights. You will not even be allowed visits from Mingus [our Siamese cat] in case you try and eat him.

The next day Jimmy took a day off so that we could go to the Blue Ridge Mountains (cue for a song . . .) in the Shenandoah Valley and, fifty miles or so from Washington, the cooler temperature of the forests provided welcome relief after the oppressive humidity in the city. We saw a solitary stag emerge from the forest and then, on a straight downhill slope, a huge wild tortoise ventured slowly onto the tarmac.

We hadn't seen another car for ages and thought we would be able to drive around it, but out of nowhere a monstrous truck zoomed towards us lights flashing, blasting its horns for all it was worth and hit the poor beast head on. Dusk was beginning to fall and it was time to head back. Looking for somewhere to eat we came across a sign advertising a restaurant and hunting lodge. Jimmy wanted to make sure it would be suitable, as we were dressed very casually.

'Out you hop! It's absolutely fine,' he said on returning, grinning broadly, 'there's a live folk band, everyone's dancing and Benny Hill is on the telly!'

Matters at the club did not improve and it was only a question of time before the enterprise folded and a very worried Jimmy returned to England later that summer. During the Goaldigger Ball at the Dorchester on 17 September 1981 the news filtered through that the American venture had imploded.

Adding salt to the wound, Elton John, who was at the time chairman of Watford FC, and who was doing the cabaret unfortunately had to pull out at the last moment. Heroically Jimmy continued to perform his duties as MC with aplomb. When he grabbed the mic and announced the bad news to the room that, due to unforeseen circumstances, Elton was indisposed, Tom Wilson leapt up from his chair and offered to give £100 if he was allowed to sing 'Bye Bye Blackbird'. The band struck up and Tom gave his own, whimsical rendition to loud cheers. Within seconds of singing the last note, the West Ham table clubbed together and Trevor Brooking sang, 'I'm Forever Blowing Bubbles', swiftly followed by Alan Minter, the boxer, doing a musical turn. A stampede for the microphone guaranteed that a lot of money went into the pot, and the spontaneous show of amateur talent, generosity triumphed over disaster.

The news of the financial demise of WSA devastated Jimmy, as so many people were involved – Coventry City alone were quoted as losing nigh on £600,000. Mike Murphy (who was a guest at the ball) was taken in by Jimmy's brave face, and was obviously under the impression that he was handling the situation. In the same article by Jim Crace mentioned above, he is quoted as saying, 'Jimmy was relaxed about the whole thing. Who can tell what goes on in his head? But, as far as I could tell, he didn't let it worry him. He did what he always does when he has a setback. He dusted himself down and started again.'

I knew it wasn't the case.

In spite of Elton's inability to be there that night he was a very supportive, hands-on member of the Goaldigger Council and staged fundraising concerts at the Empire Pool at Wembley and the Hammersmith Odeon. The latter, another complete sell-out, was on 14 December 1982, but before things got under way, Elton came out on stage and made this announcement: 'I'm sorry, but we've had a bit of bad luck today. We've just found out that our drummer can't play. But we'll soldier on.' He added that those who wished could have a refund on their tickets.

Nigel Olsson, the musician in question, had eaten an iffy takeaway earlier in the day and was miserably confined to his hotel room, but in true gung-ho theatrical spirit, and as promised by Elton, the show went on. We were there that night and were totally mesmerised by the eccentric performance of percussionist Ray Cooper. A multi-talented actor and session player who had played with most of the greats of the music world and on nearly all Elton's records, he more than made up for the lack of timpani. At the end of the evening I doubt for one moment that anyone asked for their money back. Sometime later Elton wrote and produced a 45-rpm single, 'The Goaldiggers Song', to promote awareness of the charity. Only five hundred copies were made, with the flip side a conversation between Jimmy, Eric Morecambe and Brian Moore. We had a couple, which I sold on eBay, giving the proceeds to Help for Heroes.

A month after Jimmy's football foray in America went belly-up, Ross Jenkins (ex-Watford striker), wrote to Jimmy: 'I write to thank you for paying up my contract with Washington Diplomats. Although I am obviously not familiar with the exact financial situation regarding the American venture, I know that funds were hard to come by and I appreciate the fact that the players were looked after. I regret that it was not a success and hope that Coventry have a marvellous season to compensate you. What about Coventry for the FA Cup?'

18

Out of the Frying Pan into the Fire

If you can dream – and not make dreams your master;
If you can think – and not make thoughts your aim;
If you can meet with Triumph and Disaster
And treat those two impostors just the same;
If you can bear to hear the truth you've spoken
Twisted by knaves to make a trap for fools,
Or watch the things you gave your life to, broken,
And stoop and build 'em up with worn-out tools
—from Rudyard Kipling, *If*

In July 1982 Spain was host to the World Cup Final, and Jimmy was there for the duration. Parallel to the competition a tour was being organised from England, with John Barnwell as manager and Jack Taylor as referee, for a series of charity fixtures in South Africa, which included Ossie Ardiles and Mario Kempes from Spurs. From the outset the project was super-charged with controversy since FIFA had a worldwide ban on all football contact with the country. Lawrie McMenemy, who was part of the BBC line-up in Spain, was approached to head the team (others who had been asked before-hand having refused). He couldn't accept for the simple reason that he was manager of Southampton FC, and his club was due to commence its pre-season training. This being the case, he was asked to see if Jimmy would be willing to go to South Africa.

Lawrie told me that Jimmy picked up the gauntlet without hesitating a second because he felt a 'categorical imperative to help'. In his view, 'football was for everybody, with no discrimination', and if he could achieve something towards that end, he would 'do his damnedest to bring it about'. Jimmy looked upon football as one big family around the world and, if he could bring it back together, he would – his ultimate intention being 'to remove the politics and get back into sport'.

These long-standing sentiments were endorsed way back in February 1964 in an interview with Neville Foulger from *Football Post and News*:

> I believe that the secret lies in making soccer a family entertainment. That's what we have tried to do at Coventry [he was manager at the time] and we still have a long way to go. These days you have to try and attract the man, his wife and the child to the ground. I am convinced that the key to bigger attendances is the mother. If you can get her to the game by providing comfort and enjoyment at the ground then crowds will improve.

Jimmy wasted no time in trying to get the tour sanctioned and laid the proposal in front of Sir Bert Millichip, chairman of the Football Association, who was also in Spain for the World Cup with an FA delegation. Sir Bert agreed to put it to the committee and promised to let Jimmy have an answer. Italy beat Brazil in the final 3–2 and Jimmy flew back to the UK still with no response from the FA.

That weekend we were in Sussex staying with my mother, and no one would have had the slightest suspicion that Jimmy was on the verge of having to make a life-changing decision: would we be going back to Spain for our summer holiday, or would it be to the hornets' nest in South Africa? I took a snap of the two of them on the sunny Sunday morning sitting side by side in the garden having breakfast, the table covered with newspapers, and Jimmy sporting a 'Spain '82' T-shirt.

On Monday, regardless of persistent silence from Lancaster Gate, Jimmy booked a flight to Johannesburg. He did so before the FA made their ruling in order that, as he said, 'I would at least have the chance to visit the country and make my own assessment of the issues involved'. When the FA finally contacted him, it was to tell him it was refusing to endorse the tour.

His actions are best explained by one of his oldest friends. Twelve months previously, on 30 August 1981, in an article by Alan Hubbard in the *Sunday Express* magazine, John Bromley (Head of Sport,

London Weekend Television) summed up Jimmy's personality with this honest, back-handed compliment: 'I've always said that he was born with an ego, which is his greatest strength, but also his greatest weakness because people don't understand it. People get ridiculously envious of him because he is actually very talented and has this tremendous vision. I don't think there is an ounce of malice in the man.'

Jimmy spoke at a press conference during his brief stay in South Africa: 'I ask you to understand that all those involved in this issue all love the game of football.' Ardiles echoed Jimmy's sentiments: 'The players are happy to be here, like to play as well as they can, for all to enjoy the football.'

Although in South Africa for 48 hours, he managed to take in a game of golf and a six-a-side training session (scoring the winning goal), it was pandemonium when he put a foot back on English soil. He told the waiting media that he had gone there purely in a 'consultancy capacity'. Later, in an interview with Ian Todd, journalist for the *Sun Sport*, he said, 'I believe in the players' rights to play in South Africa and I believe FIFA are wrong to exclude South Africa from international soccer. The game here is multi-racial.'

Jimmy was in trouble both with the FA and with the BBC, even though they had issued a statement, quoted in an article by a *Sports Mirror* reporter on 17 July 1981, that 'Jimmy has done nothing that violates his contract. He is employed as a freelance.' Nevertheless, an urgent summons came for Jimmy to present himself on the top floor of Television Centre where, accompanied by his agent Bagenal Harvey, he was made to apologise and the FA cleared him of any breach of regulations.

That evening I received a panic-stricken telephone call from the bar at BBC Kensington House from a very worried Bob Abrahams (editor, *Match of the Day*): 'Miss B, you'd better come quickly and pick up the old boy. He's in a bad way.'

I rushed to Shepherd's Bush and found Jimmy grey-faced, his eyes red-rimmed. The press cooled down, the dust settled, and Bags (his affectionate name for his agent) continued to have a weekly bet with his wife every Saturday night as to what colour suit his star client would be wearing on the programme.

19

Variety is the Spice of Life

Robert Winsor MBE, the 'multi-millionaire charity king', has raised countless thousands of pounds to provide wheelchairs and other vital equipment for underprivileged children in the United Kingdom and on the island of Mallorca, where he has now made his home. Back in the Eighties Robert lived in Totteridge, North London, surrounded by four acres of landscaped gardens, including a private zoo – complete with flamingos and a lake – and where, in August 1983, after his annual fundraising golf tournament held nearby, everyone was invited back for a party.

Jimmy, who had been playing in the competition, after a quick wash and brush up, headed straight for the do, whereas I was to make my way there by tube from Notting Hill. It was going to be a long evening, as there was also to be entertainment, provided by Robert's then wife, the singer Grace Kennedy and, as I didn't want to leave Ulla on her own for such a long period, she came too. When I arrived Jimmy was chatting with James 'the Shunt' Hunt (1.85 metres of pure blond gorgeousness – how *did* he squeeze all that into an F1 McLaren?), his Alsatian Oscar beside him on the grass. About to head for the buffet, I asked if they could hold fire for five minutes so that I could feed Ulla. I had brought a tin of her food and went off to find the kitchen, where Grace provided me with a can opener and a bowl. James had not come similarly prepared and filched a large steak from the barbecue, declaring, 'Chum gives Oscar the trots.'

Old friends Ron and Vee Shaw were keen fans of motor racing. In October 1985 they invited us to lunch at their home in Fawkham, Kent before going to see the Grand Prix at nearby Brands Hatch, then back again for supper. Nelson Piquet (originally from Brazil and arguably one of the greatest Formula 1 drivers ever, father of seven and teller of naughty jokes, including one involving an elephant's 'pennis' [*sic*]) was competing, staying the night with the Shaws after the race.

Unfortunately, that afternoon the three times World Champion only managed a few laps before he had to retire. During supper I mentioned that I understood a racing driver's hands could become very sore through gripping the wheel. 'Does this happen to you?' I quizzed Nelson in all innocence. Jimmy burst out laughing. 'Don't be daft. He wasn't out there long enough!'

By 1983 Jimmy and I were well and truly glued at the hip and he proposed a charity golfing jolly to Marbella. The group of celebs was flying out on the Saturday morning, and I was due to go with them, but Jimmy couldn't leave until after he had presented *Match of the Day*, and he was aware that I would struggle travelling without him to hold my hand.

Jerry Stevens, a television comedian who had been part of a comedy duo with Lennie Bennett, ran the Variety Club of Great Britain Golfing Society. When Jerry's family came to this country from Italy they opened a restaurant. His mother spoke very little English and, if someone ordered a rare steak, she got round the problem by shouting down the dumb waiter to the kitchen below, 'One-a steak-a, wella done-a – NO!'

Jimmy picked up the phone. 'Tell me, Jerry, who else is on the trip?'

'Right, let's have a look. Tim Brooke-Taylor, Richard O'Sullivan, Babs and Robert Powell ... Mick McManus?'

'Great. Give us Mick's number, there's a love.'

Born William George Matthews, Mick McManus was known professionally as 'The Man They/You Love to Hate' and 'The Dulwich Destroyer', and became arguably the biggest name in wrestling Britain has ever known. Every Saturday afternoon in the mid-Sixties my father and I used to tune in to *World of Sport* on our black-and-white set, transfixed by the bouts between legends such as Giant Haystacks, Kendo Nagasaki (he really was scary), Big Daddy (proper name: Shirley Crabtree) and, of course, Mick – my all-time number one favourite.

Quite extraordinarily, ten minutes after writing this paragraph I have just put down a copy of the *Daily Mail* '*Weekend*' magazine

(17 May 2014), which featured the article 'My Haven – Sir Peter Blake'. Under Item 3 Sir Peter says:

> I've always loved wrestling and remember my mum taking me to Bexleyheath to see Mick McManus in 1947. Then in 1975, I made a film with the legendary Kendo Nagasaki. In the film Kendo fought Giant Haystacks and was supposed to win, but Haystacks threw Kendo from the ring breaking two of his ribs. Kendo knew he couldn't win so we made Haystacks tear off Kendo's mask, which was illegal, and he lost. Afterwards Kendo gave the mask to me.

In the ensuing days, I hooked up with Jerry's wife. Rather than waste four or five hours on the course, we opted to relax on the beach. When it was my turn to get the drinks I had to pass by a group of blokes sitting at a table by the bar. I was conscious of only wearing a one-piece bathing suit which failed to cover my wobbly bits, and to my dismay, one of them started to whistle Laurel and Hardy's theme tune, 'Di dumty dum, di dumty dum, dumptity dum, di dumty dum.' Men can be so cruel ...

Jimmy took me several times to see the Horse of the Year Show, including once when he was actually competing (for charity) in December 1983 – more than thirty years ago. The horse (a frisky mount which had been lent by the barracks in Knightsbridge), unseated Jimmy. Some years later in the mid-1980s, for Christmas I presented him with a copy of *Handley Cross: or, Mr Jorrocks's Hunt* by R. S. Surtees in which I wrote: 'To my dearest Christmas pudding! See page 367 in memory of Olympia '83. From your ever loving hunt follower, B xxxxx'.

The words in my dedication refer to our hero Mr Jorrocks when he found himself in similar circumstances on the hunting field:

> Ramming the spurs into his horse, which the animal acknowledged by a sudden and desperate kick, fairly shot our master over its head. Great was the consternation! 'Hurt?' exclaimed Mr Jorrocks, his eyes sparkling with rage, as he scrambled up and replaced his lost head-gear, '*hurt*, Sir?' he repeated, looking

as though he would eat him, '*No, Sir – not at all – rather the contrary!*' Our hero, however, having fallen both clean and soft, and having vented his anger upon his non-paying subscriber, things soon resumed their right course.

When history repeated itself that night, the 'paying subscribers' loved every minute!

Another time we were guests of the BBC, the dress code black tie. I had very little cash to splash and decided the time was right to dust down my old Singer sewing machine. Fortunately I didn't have to buy any material, as I had a length of fabric lying in the bottom of a drawer a girlfriend had given me before I left France. It came from a factory which supplied the House of Dior and was a soft, floppy jersey silk covered in gold sequins. Less was definitely more in this case, and after a couple of days' hard graft I produced an ankle-skimming sheath.

Jimmy came to collect me and we drove to Hammersmith, but when we started to walk through the exhibition complex I had the unnerving feeling that I was undergoing a severe wardrobe mal-function as the garment had taken on a life of its own and, with each step, began to trail on the ground. Thankfully, as I was wearing a belt, I hoicked it up but, throughout the evening, it stretched by at least another four inches. Because of the weight of the material, I should have let it hang before stitching the hem.

I was impressed to see who Jimmy was on first-name terms with – Harvey Smith, Nick Skelton, the Whittaker brothers and David Broome, among others. Backstage we bumped into Ted Edgar, an endearing old rascal, whose idea of bareback riding was to sit in the saddle without a shirt. It was Ted's wife Liz (David Broome's sister) who had originally taught Jimmy to ride at their stables in the Mid-lands when he was manager of Coventry and they have remained firm friends ever since.

Ted gave an outrageous wink. 'If only James could choose 'is 'orses the way he chooses 'is women!'

We live less than 25 minutes from Plumpton racecourse and we were invited by the owner to join him in his box. On the morning of our trip, I selected a silk chiffon blouse in a delicate shade of peach that Jimmy had bought me in Paris when he took me there for my birthday. Unfortunately my white underwear was clearly visible through the thin fabric. Determined not to be defeated, I boiled the kettle, brewed some very strong coffee, soaked said bra until it reached the desired shade, gave it a quick rinse under the cold tap and dried it on the Aga. Perfect. Under pressure to leave in time, Jimmy said, 'Can I smell coffee?' I explained what I had done and ever the king of one-liners, he said, 'In that case, you'd better be careful in case someone tries to dunk their digestive!'

20

Another Year, Another FA Diary

The year 1984 was exceptionally busy and nearly every day the diary had more than one appointment – if not several. Jimmy's soft timbre is ideally suited for radio and he originated and hosted *Team Choice*, a programme on Radio 4. It comprised a series of recorded interviews with a range of interesting people, including the Marquis of Bath and those employed to run Longleat, the crew on a round trip to New York on Concorde, traders at the Stock Exchange – or was it employees at the Royal Mint? – the heart surgery contingent at Harefield Hospital, the Welsh National Opera and finally – real boys' stuff – the McLaren racing team.

His radio career blossomed and he was asked to front *Start the Week* (also on Radio 4), the phone-in sports programme the *606 Show*, and *Summer Sounds* on Radio 2, broadcast live on Sunday afternoons from quintessentially English venues such as Henley Regatta and the All England Jumping Course at Hickstead. Frankie Vaughan (best remembered for his high kicks when singing 'Give Me the Moonlight', and for whom Jimmy played on many of his charity golf days on behalf of Boys' Clubs) wrote in April: 'Heard you "chairing" *Start the Week* and the Concorde interview on Radio [4]. Both very professional jobs. Congratulations.'

In 1961 Jimmy was asked by his old school to contribute to the Old Thorntonians' newsletter. Introduced as Chairman of the Professional Footballers' Association, he wrote:

My first term at Thornton's was to have started in September 1939, but Hitler plotted a war and my mother and father schemed my evacuation to Chichester without my knowledge. I was marooned with boys from Chichester High School, but six months later, as soon as the South-West London Emergency Secondary School opened, I was able, by subtle argument and more effective tearful demonstration, to force my way back to the capital.

Douglas Bunn, the master of Hickstead, was a full-time pupil at the school in Sussex and while he and his contemporaries used the classroom in the morning the evacuees from London in the afternoon, the two men only met when they were adults.

Billeted first in Pagham, then in the cathedral city itself, an 11-year-old Jimmy missed his family desperately. He returned to Balham just as the Blitz began in earnest – except his 'own little bed', as per the lyrics of the song 'The White Cliffs of Dover', turned out having to share an Anderson shelter in the back garden every night with seven other family members.

Many years later, living five minutes away from Douglas's country estate, we were frequently invited to join him along with Ned Sherrin, Caryl Brahms (author of *No Bed for Bacon*, thought to be the inspiration for the film *Shakespeare in Love*), Orson Welles' daughter Beatrice, Dame Vera Lynn and Dai 'seducer of the Valleys' Llewellyn in his private pavilion overlooking the Hickstead arena. The Princess Royal was there on one occasion with her daughter Zara, a close friend of the Bunns' youngest, Daisy. Still in their school uniforms, the two little girls beetled off to investigate the trade stands, returning half an hour later, Daisy delighted with the novelty watch she had bought.

'Can I have one too, please, Mummy?' Zara asked politely.

'No.'

'Why?'

'What did I say?'

'"No", Mummy.'

'Then there are no supplementary questions', the Princess Royal declared with a twinkle in her eye.

Zara trotted off perfectly happily, confident within the boundaries set by a very caring, loving – and sensible – parent.

In March the Variety Club Golfing Society organised the Jimmy Tarbuck Classic in southern Spain. Still an innocent abroad, I hadn't stayed in many hotels and was impressed on arrival to see a complimentary bottle of Cava chilling in an ice bucket in our room. I unpacked our cases and ten minutes later I found Jimmy up to his ears in hot water scrubbing the mud off his golf clubs so they would be pristine on the first tee next day and just like me, they were relegated to the uncomfortable tap end of the bath.

Exactly three years before, in 1981, Jimmy had been granted permission by the Jockey Club Licensing Committee to ride in the third running of the Mad Hatters' Private Sweepstakes at Plumpton. Unfortunately, due to commitments, he had to cancel at the last moment, but in 1984, he had another chance to take part in the sport of kings, this time at Sandown on a horse called Luckliffe.

Sponsored by the Formula One Constructors' Association, the competition was to raise funds for the Dyslexia Foundation. The ultimate athlete, Jimmy took training to heart and gave up alcohol to help lose those extra pounds. The week before the race we had been invited to the Chelsea Arts Club ball at the Royal Albert Hall, but before we could let our hair down, Jimmy had to get *Match of the Day* under his belt, and by the time we arrived (approaching midnight) everyone was well and truly oiled – and three sheets plus VAT – to the wind.

We leaned over the balcony of our box sober as a couple of po-faced judges and observed the revellers on the dance floor below, wondering if we were that silly when we spliced the mainbrace. The orchestra struck up a slow waltz – about my speed – and Jimmy asked me to dance. After we had negotiated our way down to the lower level a couple sidled over to us, clearly the worse for wear. The lady, of generous proportions and resembling the *Black Pearl* in full sail, prodded Jimmy on the chest. 'You might be an effing television presenter,' she slurred, tripping on her words, not the light fantastic, 'but you can't effing dance!'

We felt it was time to make our excuses and went our separate ways to the loo before the journey home. In the cooler calm of the cloakroom, while I was washing my hands, I cast an eye to my left and noticed a stylish woman of a certain age who seemed familiar. Did I know her? If I did, for the life of me I couldn't remember her name. What if she recognised me first? It was only later that the penny dropped and I realised that I had been sharing the Albert Hall Ladies' with Lauren Bacall, Mrs Humphrey Bogart.

To finish the original story, with the support of John Oaksey, Jimmy did run in the race and, although not the first past the winning post, by not coming last in no way did he disgrace himself.

Jimmy deftly shoehorned me into the Saturday lunches at Oliver's restaurant in Holland Park with his colleagues from the BBC, including Jim Reside (now producer, *Ski Sunday*), Alistair Scott (senior sports director), Martin Hopkins (Head of Major Events, BBC Sport), 'Big' Bob Wilson (ex-Arsenal goalkeeper and co-presenter on *Match of the Day*) and 'Little' Bob Abrahams (editor, *Match of the Day*).

When Gary Lineker began presenting *Football Focus*, he joined the group. After lunch Jimmy went to the studios to watch the matches relayed from the grounds and, the scripts written and running order in place, retired to the bar, where he had a tradition that, for every goal Coventry scored, he would sink a glass of Ruddles ale. Lively stuff, Ruddles! A major panic arose at one of the get-togethers at Oliver's when the lads realised, with very few shopping days left before Christmas, that they needed to buy gifts for the girls back at the office. Could I bale them out? I asked what sort of presents they were thinking of buying. 'Easy,' Little Bob said, 'a pair of goalkeeping gloves and a dildo.'

'I have absolutely no problem with the dildo,' I offered, 'but I'm afraid I draw the line at goalkeeping gloves!'

21

Foot Faults

Jimmy was an excellent tennis player and when we first met he belonged to the Queen's Club in Barons Court, West London and the David Lloyd Centre near Heathrow. In March 1958 in an article entitled 'Eagle SPORTS News' he wrote, 'Now take tennis. Admittedly there is no chance in singles to capture team spirit and all it entails, but on the other hand, there is no one else to help you do a job. You're out there on your own.'

He started playing with a group of Hungarians and, if Puskás came to shove, one would struggle to find a more rambunctious bunch of rapscallions this side of the Danube. Jimmy wasn't a regular betting man, but the mid-Europeans started a book as soon as they were in the dressing room. Most of them were of undeclared marital status, and sometimes a variety of girlfriends made up the party for the post-match suppers. I became friendly with one of them who – like me – was considerably younger than her own *amour*. Fully aware that his affections were perhaps not as exclusive as she would have wished, I found her attitude refreshing when she assured me that she didn't mind 'vot Tibor gets up to during the day, as long as I'm the one who gives him breakfast in de mornink'.

To keep me occupied, Jimmy promised me an hour's coaching with Onny Parun. Originally from Croatia, Onny was brought up in New Zealand and played in their Davis Cup team. Tall, lean and handsome, at one point he was in the world top twenty, and he reached the quarterfinals at Wimbledon in 1972. 'Let's see what you can do,' he suggested in his lilting Antipodean accent. After ten minutes of hitting balls fast and furiously at me he approached the net. 'Well, Bryony, there's absolutely nothing I can do with your backhand.'

Occasionally I used to be called upon to make up the four in mixed doubles at home. 'Go up to the net . . . Nearer . . . Bit more. Fine. Stop! Don't move!' Jimmy shouted at me, giving him carte blanche to run around as if playing singles. However, when a ball happened in my direction he would yell, 'Yours!' for me to slam it home, the element of surprise and my lethal dolly-drop serve our secret weapons.

One summer we went to France with Tom and Heather, driving down to the Dordogne, where we stayed in a splendid hotel built into the rock face in Les Eyzies-de-Tayac-Sireuil, the cavernous home of Cro-Magnon man. We were told at reception that if we collected the key from the chemist we could play on the municipal court a short walk away.

Tom used his racquet as if it was a cricket bat (more his game) and played forward. Unused to such searing heat, the four of us struggled and returned exhausted with steam coming out of our ears. The proprietor, in spite of the temperature, sported a magnificent beard *à la* Capitaine Haddock (Tintin's best friend) and a cardigan over a well-fed tummy, a good indication of the quality of the cooking of the establishment. He took one look at our scarlet faces.

'*Mon dieu*,' he said in astonishment, 'you Eengleesh. Zees ees not 'olidays. Zees ees work!'

I always believed that Jimmy suggested using the Royal Albert Hall as a venue for the Rothmans International Tennis Tournament in March 1970 when Rod Laver, Ken Rosewall, John Newcombe, Roger Taylor and others battled it out on a specially laid carpet. Years later, when Jimmy was due to play in a charity competition at the same venue, he was drawn to partner Patrick McEnroe (John's younger brother) against Sir Cliff Richard (an excellent tennis player) alongside Peter Fleming. Jimmy asked Patrick what their tactics were – that is, should they go for it or, as it was supposedly a friendly, behave like gentleman? 'Okay', Patrick replied, 'it may be for a good cause, Jim, but we're definitely here to win', concluding that, at 1.92m, Peter had an 'altitude problem.'

Sir Terry Wogan shared the same view. 'Losing was never an option for Jimmy. When I played tennis against him [again at the Royal Albert Hall] he took great pleasure in "aceing" me with a swinging serve. Good friends we might have been, but this was a game – and Jimmy wanted to win!'

By not flaunting our friendship we had managed to keep our names out of the tabloids, but a party given in November 1984 by Michael Barratt to celebrate his forty years in newspapers and television put paid to our privacy. Dressed in a black taffeta skirt, a white satin blouse with a floppy bow and pearls, I stuck to Jimmy like a limpet. Although four years before the launch of *Hello!* Magazine, it was normal for photographers to be present, and a few days later a picture of us appeared in the William Hickey column of the *Daily Express*. 'Jimmy signs a new team-mate,' the caption read. Not long afterwards, when I arrived at the office, having bought my paper from the shop next door, I spotted another photographer further down Westbourne Grove suspiciously manhandling an obscenely large telephoto lens.

A second article hit the press, this time in Nigel Dempster's column in the *Daily Mail*, stating that Jimmy 'maintained' another household in London. Since I was paying for everything, we sought legal advice, which resulted in a printed apology. Although in no way to blame, Michael B was very concerned about the problems the exposure had caused and invited us to a special showing of *Starlight Express* in the presence of Princess Diana.

22

From Golf Course to Cathedral

In February 1985 Sir Bernard Audley lent us his apartment in Soto-grande, southern Spain. Bernard invented the expression 'situational etiquette'. Imagine you are at the Berkshire Golf Club, your partner preparing to hit his ball on the first tee, when your dog (an almost obligatory item for the members) goes and sits behind him. If you say nothing and your companion continues with his down swing you run the risk of losing your faithful hound. On the other hand, do you interrupt what could have been the tee shot of a lifetime and risk losing a friend?

Tim Brooke-Taylor recounted the following story that I'd forgotten about.

I have many happy memories of Jimmy. He has always been fun, generous and an outstanding good egg. We had a lot of good times together with SPARKS and other charity sports days but a picture I will always have in my mind is a face-off, or rather a chin-off between Jimmy and Bruce Forsyth. I cried, 'chins up' and they both raised their chins as I sailed through, as if they were two halves of Tower Bridge.

Jimmy very kindly asked my wife Christine and me to play golf at the wonderful Berkshire Golf course. A lot of players at the Berkshire wear red cords and have a dog. Jimmy didn't have the cords, but he had the dog – George. George sat patiently by the first tee. He watched our drives, then disappeared, presumably out of sheer embarrassment. We didn't see him again until the eighteenth green where he arrived just in time for a drink at the nineteenth hole.

Little Bob came with us to Sotogrande so that the chaps could enjoy a round of golf on the famous course close to the border with Portugal. They also planned to play at another course near Marbella, but on that particular morning the heavens opened in monsoon proportions. Nevertheless, we set off in the hope that the weather might improve. While Bob was ordering coffees at the bar a Rupert Bear lookalike dressed in yellow trousers, a red sweater and white golf shoes spotted us and sauntered over.

'Well I never, fancy seeing you here,' Jimmy said to 'Rupert', 'would you believe, it's Miss B's birthday!'

All of a sudden I was scooped up in a pair of powerful arms and given a kiss, not by Bill Badger's best chum, but by none other than Sean Connery ... Oh, oh heaven.

In an interview on 13 March 1985 with Penny Faust for Radio Oxford Jimmy said, 'Most people know the ending to *Macbeth* and some to *La Traviata* but there is instant drama every week on *Match of the Day*.'

He liked to say that if a player had a difficult name to pronounce he had to have a heck of a good game to get a mention on the programme. He also said (for fun) that, when times were bad, Coventry players should sport their numbers on the front of their shirts so that everyone thought they were attacking.

I found this draft for an article, which encapsulates Jimmy's passion for the game:

For me, football means a job but it's also my favourite hobby. This magic game has brought so much pleasure to so many people in different ways. To some it means just a once-a-week chance of winning a fortune on the pools, [but] the luckiest in my view are those who play, or have played, to a reasonable standard. The days I played for Fulham and Brentford were the most enjoyable of my life, everything else I have done since has been a substitute for playing. Yet I know many fanatical supporters of League clubs whose pleasure at just being involved is enormous.

To some, it's almost a substitute for religion – the ground is the church, the battle songs the hymns. It's a common language, sadly sometimes the only language that fathers and sons can speak together, but what a blessing that can be. But for the fun we get it's only fair we should play our part by putting something back into football. The game never stands still.

It will be different this season in the Football League – slight changes going on all the time. The Chinese play the same game in another way, as do the South Americans, the Arabs, and before long, the North Americans will develop their own style. Throughout the world it's a never-ending struggle to achieve perfection. We've still got much to learn from other countries, as they have learned things from us. But if you don't find out how good you really are you'll never get better. To establish the truth is essential.

On 21 April 1985 we were lucky enough to go to the British pre-miere of Andrew Lloyd-Webber's *Requiem* at Westminster Abbey performed by Sarah Brightman, Placido Domingo and the wunder-kind boy soprano Paul Miles-Kingston. It was a very cold winter's day and, with the anti-fur campaign PETA still in its infancy, I wore a mink coat, which I bought myself, thus refuting the saying my mother used to quote: 'Minks get minks the way girls get minks.' Our seats were right up at the front of the abbey adjacent to the singers' podium, the orchestra so close we could have tugged at their coat tails. Halfway into a moving solo by Placido something living emerged from my lapel, flew upwards and fluttered past the poor man's face. Mimicking Peter Sellers in the role of Inspector Clouseau, Jimmy whispered in my ear, '*Meuth.*'

23

Horses for Courses

Jimmy kept a horse, an Appaloosa called Buchan. Also called Spotty Bottom (because of the irregular patterns on his coat typical of the breed), he was a noble beast and became a popular character in the Cotswold riding community. From early autumn Jimmy's mind turned to the thrills and spills of the hunting field and he drove weekly from Notting Hill to the Midlands to ride with hounds. The Heythrop (of whom he was a member) is 'Wednesday country' and there was always a mad rush to get back to the BBC in time if it was his turn to front that evening's football programme, *Sportsnight*. Although he was a courageous and experienced horseman, one day, a rogue branch sent him flying from the saddle.

The extent of his injuries was more serious than he realised, nearly passing out in the bath with the pain. An hour into the journey to London disaster struck a second time when, on changing gear, he was hit by a wave of excruciating agony. He had dislocated his shoulder in the fall, and the sideways movement slotted the joint back into its socket.

The editor of the programme, on seeing that his front man was deathly pale, summoned the BBC doctor from his armchair, who diagnosed a suspected fractured collarbone in addition to the dislocation. With a *whoosh* of adrenalin Jimmy insisted on carrying out the transmission, the only concession to his injury being that he appeared with his arm in a sling. The next day X-rays confirmed a break and the orthopaedic surgeon, (a QPR supporter), booked Jimmy in at the old Charing Cross Hospital in Fulham Palace Road for an operation – but not before he – Jimmy, not the doc. – had presented *Match of the Day* on Saturday night. What a super trouper.

The unpredictability of live television was highlighted dramatically on the evening of Wednesday 29 May 1985. The European Cup Final between Liverpool and Juventus was due to be played at Heysel in Belgium, with Jimmy as presenter. Beforehand Terry Wogan was hosting his thrice-weekly chat show, interviewing his only guest that evening, Bruce Forsyth, and the two future knights of the realm were eagerly anticipating a victory for the home team. Approximately one hour before kick-off, violence erupted at the stadium between the Liverpool fans and their Italian rivals, a fact of which the studio in London was oblivious, not least Terry and Bruce.

Terry, in jocular mood, was linked directly to Jimmy who, seeing the chaos unfolding in front of his eyes at the Belgian stadium, had the impossible task of switching the buoyant atmosphere in London to one of somber disbelief. A retaining wall that separated the fans had collapsed, resulting in the loss of 39 lives and hundreds of injured. The extraordinary decision was taken to play the match in order to prevent further violence; Liverpool beat Juventus 1–0 with a penalty in the second half. In the aftermath the 1930s stadium was demolished and all English clubs were banned from taking part in European football for a period of five years.

24

After the Nightmare My Dream Comes True

After several years of renting, I was able to purchase the leasehold on my flat in Pembridge Crescent, but the total refurbishment that was necessary rendered us temporarily homeless. Jimmy was currently a director of Charlton Athletic FC. Sunley Holdings (the club's bene-factors) owned a block of flats in North Row off Marble Arch, and John Sunley generously gave us the key to the company apartment.

After a month of living out of suitcases Jimmy hit me with the news that he had decided to sell Harcomb, his house in the Cots-wolds, in order to set up home with me. I couldn't believe my ears – after nearly a decade of no promises of a future together, I was finally potting the black. A glossy brochure was produced, a photo appeared in *Country Life* magazine and we crossed our fingers for a quick sale.

In the meantime Jimmy had been suffering from severe back pain, which forced him to hang up his riding boots. What was to become of Buchan? With perfect timing, an offer came from Gloucestershire farmer Richard Tetley:

> Grove Farm, 21 July 1985. Ian Simpson [a neighbour] tells me that he spoke to you on my behalf about your hunter. Should you be considering selling Buchan, may I be presumptuous enough to ask you to give me the first refusal of him? Obviously, I have no idea of your plans, so this request may seem pretty impertinent but if there is an opportunity, I don't want to miss it simply because I haven't asked! I am sure Tommy [Delaney] would be prepared to give us a reference as to the quality of care our horses get here – and, if you wanted an arrangement

113

whereby you came down for an occasional day with hounds, we'd be happy to make that possible.

This was too good to be true and Jimmy responded by return. On 13 August a second letter arrived from Grove Farm:

Tommy came to see me today to pass on your very generous offer of Buchan. I am most embarrassed and extremely grateful to you for it, and I naturally accept the offer with indecent haste! I understand you are being kind enough to give me the horse on the condition that, as long as we look after him as if he was our own, we may treat him as our own, and that I never pass him on to anyone else. When he comes to the end of his days (unless by accident, which requires instant decision) you would wish me to consult with you and, in any event, he would go to the Heythrop kennels.

On 15 August another letter dropped on the mat, this time 'written' by Buchan to Mr Tetley, his new guardian:

Having met you briefly during last hunting season and hearing that you have some stable accommodation to spare at your establishment, I am taking the liberty of ask you if it is possible for me to be stabled with you for the coming hunting season. I am told that the standard is very good and that I shall be well looked after for my general feeding and sleeping arrangements by your good wife. As the weather is, and has been, very inclement this summer, I would like to take advantage of this situation fairly shortly. Any further information you may require such as my travel arrangements, please contact my agent T. Delaney, whose address and telephone number you already know. I look forward to hearing from you.

Within a short space of time Buchan was safely delivered to his new home, with correspondence now between horse and old master:

The Stables, 30 August 1985. I am settling down very well with the new people who, although not a patch on you and Mr

Delaney of course, do appear friendly. They make me walk for a long way every morning because they say I need to lose some weight. What a thing to say about a person of my age and experience! Perhaps you will come and visit me so that we can talk about old times.

In November 1985 we moved into the house of our dreams that was perfectly located for Jimmy to get to London and only minutes away from my mother. Although he was often away for days at a stretch I was blissfully happy, and the free time gave me the opportunity to paint and to learn how to grow vegetables and create a flower garden. However, my foray into landscaping caused a great deal of consternation and I was accused of removing valuable space in which he could have practised his golf shots!

I love food, I love cooking, and I can think of nothing nicer than combining both and preparing feasts for friends and family. Most of Jimmy's life centred around meeting strangers, and when we bought the house in Sussex we wanted to curl in on ourselves, battening down the hatches and mixing solely with familiar faces. Strange though it may seem, getting to know new people is hard work, and to our neighbours we must have appeared stand-offish.

One evening when Jimmy was in London Ma came round for supper. The phone rang and it was a woman who lived in the next village. She introduced herself and said that she was getting together a group of 'local girls' for coffee. Would I like to join them? It was exactly the sort of thing I had been dreading and, caught on the hop, I accepted. Ma knew exactly how I felt and, after another stiff gin I rang her back and cancelled, explaining limply my reasons for turning it down. Naturally she sounded put out and I felt awful, but at the same time relieved that I was off that particular social hook.

The months went by and, warmed by the generous welcome and kindness from our neighbours, gradually we dipped our toes into the water of village life. Jimmy, encouraged by approaches to be involved in local events, not only turned on the Christmas lights but was asked to be president of Hurst Colts, handing out the trophies to the kids at the end of every season.

Jimmy threw himself into trying to keep the A&E department open at the Princess Royal Hospital, Haywards Heath. Along with fellow Hurstpierpoint resident actress Judy Parfitt, they waged a war in which they lent their high profiles to publicise the scandal of closing such a vital facility and, to this day at any rate, it remains open. He also put his name to the battle against an incoming tsunami of red brick from developers hoping to plough up our historic woodlands and fields to build thousands of houses, and so far - thank heavens - each application has been quashed.

At one rally I was asked to say a few words and, overcome at the thought of our beautiful heritage disappearing under lorry loads of Readymix, I embarrassed myself by bursting into tears. Nick Herbert, our MP, was the next speaker, and when I handed him the microphone I apologised for my lack of composure. 'Don't worry,' he said chivalrously, 'it's an emotional topic and I have more experience at doing this sort of thing than you.'

John Snow, who played cricket for Sussex and was England's fast bowler between Fred Trueman (whose daughter Rebecca married Raquel Welch's son Damon) and Bob Willis (fast bowler who played for England), lives three miles away, and every Christmas Eve Jennifer, John's wife, would wake us up at an unearthly hour in order to drive down to the (now defunct) fruit and vegetable market in Brighton.

Jen is statuesquely beautiful and created quite a stir, but when we walked into the huge warehouse, to a man, the traders started shouting out, 'Hey! Jim's here! It must be Christmas!' Though the clock had barely struck four we were considered late arrivals. Fortunately there were still plenty of flowers and vegetables left and we bought sacks of onions and carrots, trays of avocados and oranges at less than wholesale prices, which we shared between us. Having put our purchases in the car, we called in at the all-night café for a restorative bacon sarnie and pint of tea.

At the Late Night Shopping event in December 2011 he performed his last 'official' village appearance, dressing up as one of the three kings alongside David Gold (Chairman of West Ham FC, who has a house nearby - no prizes for guessing which king he was) in the bus shelter in the High Street, which had been converted into a stable complete with donkey, sheep and goat.

25

Runners and Riders

On 22 February 1986 we received an update from Grove Farm:

> Having decided to start the roughing-off process of Buchan Hill Esq I thought you might like a brief resumé of his season's activities: in addition to several mornings' cubbing he took us hunting on 13 days - 11 with the Heythrop and one each with the Vale of Aylesbury and the Whaddon Chase. Throughout he jumped beautifully over big fences (and not so brilliantly over small ones!) and occasionally when he wasn't asked to jump at all. He refused once only, and that was entirely my fault. He never fell or parted company with his jockey, he was never lame, sick or sorry, not missing a day's exercise let alone hunting. In the stable he is the most perfect gentleman and has become a much-loved character because of it. Those bare facts, and my words, cannot do justice to - or explain - the enormous amount of fun that Buchan has given us not only in the hunting field where he excels, but also at home and out exercising - even if it's just his head poking out of the stable window greeting us when we return from going out. We understand that you named your horse after Martin Buchan [Manchester United central defender]. Perhaps one day you'll tell me how you knew the latter had a spotty bottom!

In May Jimmy travelled with the BBC to Mexico for the World Cup. By that time we had been living in Sussex for six months and it was a major wrench for us to be apart for such a long time so, pre-email, letters provided a welcome lifeline. One of these he wrote from the Sheraton Towers in Mexico City:

Dear lovely Miss B,

Mike [Murphy] gave us dinner and drinks last night, which ended with us singing in Abraham's room [Little Bob] until 3.00 am. The Mexicans were making so much noise outside we couldn't have slept anyway. I've spent a lot of time with Mike and Jonathan [Martin, BBC Head of Sport] and we've virtually never stopped telling jokes and laughing. Only two weeks to go now and there's a lot to do. My matches are in Mexico, Puebla and Monterey and I shall be flying around in our super Beechcraft jet – don't tell the papers. Yesterday's celebrations were quite wonderful and despite all their depravations the Mexicans are a happy race. We came back from the stadium in a van – 2½ hours for 5 miles but the streets were lined with cheering people, chanting, singing and whistling even the policemen and the army with machine guns. The young Mexican girls are very striking. *Pacienca*, lovely one.

Your own sweetheart,
Jimbo xxxxx

You can keep the man out of football but you can't keep football out of the man. In March 1987 Jimmy received a letter from Graham Taylor, then the manager of Watford FC:

Following the meeting at Aston Villa, I thought I would drop you a short line. I know that both of us are very busy, as indeed is Eddie Plumley [club secretary at Coventry who Jimmy sold to Elton John when he was Chairman of Watford for £15,000 – the only secretary in the history of football to be sold to another club]. I wonder if it would be possible for a bit of lunch or a spot of dinner? My reason for suggesting this is that I really do believe that the Committee of yourself, Bertie Mee [ex-manager, Arsenal] and Ron Greenwood [ex-manager of the England team] can play a tremendous part in convincing the Management Committee as to which direction to take.

Jimmy gathered together the group of football colleagues suggested by Graham Taylor plus Graham Kelly (Chief Executive of the Football Association). They called themselves the 'Improve the Game Committee', and our house was chosen as the venue for them to thrash out the current problems in the game, hoping to find solutions. In spite of my lack of interest in football it was fun being privy to history being made around our dining-room table. One day I decided to serve lunch in the more informal surroundings of the kitchen. Bertie came and stood beside me at the sink.

'Thank you,' he said, 'now I know we're part of the family.'

26

FULHAM = *Fun, Unstinting Loyalty, Hope Alongside Misunderstanding*

In March 1987 the stretch of the Thames between Hammersmith and Putney Bridges became turbulent when Ernest Clay (Yorkshire businessman, erstwhile chairman of Fulham), thanks to Tom Wilson's wise and experienced counsel (he qualified as a chartered surveyor when playing as full-back), managed to obtain the freehold interest of Craven Cottage from the Church Commissioners. This achieved, Mr Clay sold the ground.

The purchaser was Marler Estates, whose portfolio already included two other London grounds: Loftus Road (home of Queens Park Rangers, capacity 18,439, compared with Craven Cottage's 25,700) and Chelsea's patch at Stamford Bridge (capacity 41,837). With this turn of events a flaming sword of Damocles hung perilously over Fulham's future. Would Marlers wind up the club? If so, would it merge with QPR? And, if that were the case, would Craven Cottage then be released for development?

In the same month Ma and I left for New Zealand to see her mother Esme, who was about to celebrate her 90th birthday. We would be away for eighteen days, and when we left England Jimmy was hobbling about on crutches following surgery for a torn Achilles tendon contracted through a competitive game of tennis, and entrenched as a director of Charlton Athletic.

Before I left the UK I had put a couple of stamped, addressed airmail letters on the kitchen table in case he felt the urge to get in touch. In my absence, the big news hitting the headlines announced that Fulham FC was facing its nemesis; with increasing financial worries and, having sold off its leading players, the club was spiral-ling rapidly towards Division Three.

Two days after my departure Jimmy sent me a billet-doux:

My darling Miss B, I can't tell you how busy I've been. The phone never stops ringing. Marlers are proving difficult over the negotiations and we have the final 'make or break' meeting tomorrow at Tom's office at 11.45 a.m. If we reach an agree-ment it will be announced tomorrow afternoon. On Wednesday I started at 8.45 a.m. – breakfast with Gordon Taylor [Chief Executive, Professional Footballers' Association] and GK [Graham Kelly, Football Association] to discuss the code of conduct – referees from 10.30–1.20 p.m. Meeting with Tom and David Bulstrode [Chairman of Marler Estates] till 7.00 p.m. 1½ hours' drive after a jolly nice dinner, home for 10.30 p.m.: Northern Ireland v England on telly – sleep! There are signs of spring, the sun keeps coming through and little flowers are popping up everywhere. I'm still sane, but only just, and am looking forward to your return on Sunday week with eager anticipation when I see your happy, smiling facing again (with a cup of tea!). Hurry home. The house is waiting. Your loving JH, xxxxx

Ma and I flew in to Heathrow after a marathon 22-hour flight via Singapore and Dubai to be greeted by Jimmy and George, whom he had brought along for the ride. In the excitement at seeing my two boys it took a few minutes before I realised that Jimmy's leg was free of plaster. Clicking the seat belt into place, he said, 'Before we go any further, I had better tell you that I am no longer a director of Charlton. That's the good news. The bad is that I am now chairman of Fulham.'

Spinning onto the M25, Jimmy piled on the pressure. 'Oh yes, I've asked the new vice chairman Bill Muddyman and his son Andy to lunch; they're probably at the house already. I've told them you're cooking roast lamb and rhubarb crumble and custard. They can't wait!'

The Muddymans were lifelong Fulham residents and fans, and

entrepreneur Bill, the youngest of nine children, proved to be the salvation of the South London club. Living abroad at the time but still following his beloved team and all too aware of the club's precarious position, he was keen to try and help. He contacted a running buddy, David Emery (sports editor at the *Daily Express*), who said that in his view, Jimmy was the only person likely to be able to spearhead the campaign to save the club. At Bill's request, David arranged a meeting between the three of them at a restaurant in Bayswater in order to work out survival tactics.

Bill and Andy attended a further meeting at Bernard Coral's establishment, the Wig and Pen Club (delightfully misnamed the Wig and Penguin Club by one of the secretaries at Craven Cottage) in the Strand opposite the Old Bailey, near Fleet Street. Whatever funds were raised that evening Bill offered to match pound for pound on the proviso that Jimmy would be chairman 'for a period of two years', as Jimmy stated in his book. With substantial financial input from two other individuals (who were also appointed as directors of the soon-to-be-created Fulham Football Club 1987 Limited), the sum amounted to £157,000, doubling up to £314,000 when Bill fulfilled his promise. In the ensuing years, this investment rose to many millions and ultimately the freehold of Craven Cottage was preserved.

Thus began a good friendship between the Hills and the Muddymans, which lasted for almost a decade. With Jimmy as chairman and Bill and Andy contributing as directors and with further financial support, they did their best to run the club, but unfortunately this was not mirrored with the same success on the pitch.

Sadly, when personal and business relationships are cheek by jowl, difficulties can develop. The Royal Bank of Scotland had 'reluctantly' become Fulham's landlord in 1992 when Marler Estates went bust. Marler had pledged its assets to the bank as security for large loans and Craven Cottage was one of those assets. So when Marler went under, RBS acquired the ground. Tom Wilson (now on the new board at Fulham) and his fellow directors agreed a life-saving deal with the bank whereby the club was allowed to play there rent free in return for Tom, a highly regarded property man, seeking to increase the value of the ground by obtaining a planning consent for part residential development. The bank also agreed the club could buy the ground back for a fixed priced of £7.5 million.

Getting planning approval, however, proved very difficult and protracted. During this time, Tom and Jimmy kept the goodwill of the bank by keeping them informed on a regular basis. The RBS knew Tom was putting in a huge amount of work on the planning request despite his commitments as senior partner of his surveying firm, St Quintin. As a gesture of goodwill, the bank informally agreed that, in recognition of Tom's efforts, it would allow a 10% reduction on the £7.5 million price. It was a gentleman's agreement.

Bill told me that his and Andy's advisors felt strongly that the best time to strike a deal was before the planning value was realised. When the planning approval was finally confirmed Craven Cottage had suddenly become a very valuable piece of land. Tom's hard work and strong relationship with the bank had created the value but the Muddyman family had also bankrolled the club through its terrible financial times. Between them they had all kept Fulham alive.

When the stakes became higher and, more importantly, as Bill told me, their family money was put at risk, the widening commercial and strategic difference in approach became glaringly apparent. Valiant attempts were made to maintain a united front but the Muddymans naturally wanted to be in control, since they were the ones who put up the funds.

On a brighter note, there was better news from the pitch. In April 1997 Jimmy received a letter from Sir James Wilkinson KBE MC DI:

My warmest congratulations on Fulham's promotion to the Second Division. It has been a memorable season but, as you will know better than I, not a particularly easy one despite the success in getting promotion. I am so pleased, in particular, for you since I know how much of your own time and energy you have invested in keeping Fulham FC going and in achieving this promotion. Very many congratulations on a well deserved success, which will have given great pleasure to very many people in Fulham, apart from myself.

Discord between Jimmy, Bill and Andy increased behind the scenes and, although in spirit their objectives remained the same, their strategies were poles apart and Jimmy failed to win the internal commercial battle when he insisted that the best tactical approach was going forward with RBS.

Jimmy and Tom met the RBS shortly after planning had been finalised. They asked for an even bigger reduction although the bank would have been fully entitled to insist on the full £7.5 million. But the RBS kept its word and agreed to sell the ground back to the club for £6.75 million and Jimmy and Tom agreed for the club to buy it back at that price. The deal went through fairly promptly, only for the ground and the club to be sold on almost at once.

Tom and Jimmy were unaware of the on-sale and were distraught. The bank had honoured its word. Tom had kept to his word. Tom and Jimmy had done their very best to preserve the club, and had succeeded, but had unknowingly delivered it into what turned out to be a very safe pair of hands.

With great sadness, the resulting fall out culminated in the Muddymans formally removing Jimmy and Tom from Fulham's board.

Fulham did indeed return to its rightful place among football's elite in the Premiership – an achievement which couldn't have been reached without the help of the Muddymans. Having bought the freehold, they provided a firm foundation on which the club was able to rebuild its reputation.

Unfortunately, life is never an easy ride and, since the last change of ownership in 2013, Fulham has experienced another downturn in its fortunes. 'But,' as Bill told me, 'hope springs eternal and, if Fulham fans are anything, they are always hopeful!'

In May 1997, shortly after Jimmy stepped down as chairman, he received a letter from Barbara Bowden, whose words expressed the feelings of many of the supporters:

In the ten years you have been our chairman you have always shown me the utmost courtesy when I came into the directors' room to sell you and your guests lottery tickets. The last ten years have been the most emotionally exhausting times and you and your board have remained constant. I cried again on 1 May when Mr Muddyman announced that the board had regained the freehold. This season has been so rewarding, I believe it even tops 1974-75. I salute your decision to leave when everything is beginning to fall into place. You said you would only stay for a few years and have shown integrity in remaining at the helm in bad times.

27

Plays, Parties and Purple

We weren't huge theatregoers, but nevertheless we endeavoured to see as many plays and musicals as we could find the time to, including most of the Andrew Lloyd-Webber/Tim Rice productions. In June 1987 Jimmy booked tickets for us to see *Les Misérables*, which had been running for a few seasons. He asked the taxi driver to take him to the Queen's Theatre.

'Seeing it again, Jim?'

'No, it's the first time.'

'Blimey, guv, you've left it a bit late.'

That November Rick Wakeman asked us to the annual SODS (Society of Distinguished Songwriters) dinner in London when Marty Wilde (popular singer and songwriter in the Sixties and father of 'Kids in America' pop star Kim) was to be crowned King Sod. According to tradition, his wife had to make a speech at his inauguration. Joyce (one of the original Vernons Girls) was brilliant and proved a thoroughly entertaining speaker, concluding with the immortal words, 'At our age we've reached the point in our lives that when we turn out the light there's more of us outside the bed than in it!'

The following July we were guests of the Gallaher tobacco group at the Silk Cut Derby at Hickstead and, after watching the jumping from the marquee by the course and enjoying a splendid lunch and tea, we returned home. Minutes later the phone rang. It was Lorna Bunn pleading for us to come to their after-derby party, which she advised was fancy dress, the purple Silk Cut livery the theme. We are not ones for dressing up and, after a busy social day, we didn't think we'd bother and were looking forward to a peaceful evening at home. Lorna was insistent, however, and so we agreed.

I searched the house high and low and succeeded in unearthing a purple-striped shirt for Jimmy. The bottom half proved more difficult; I dug out an ancient similarly coloured pair of shorts and black velvet slippers embroidered with foxes, which loosely covered the horsey side of things. As for me, I found a length of mauve material and, with a snip here and there, made it into a sort of tunic/toga thingy, securing it with a matching sash.

Slipping on lilac espadrilles, I went into the garden and picked a load of purple sweet peas, which I threaded into garlands, one for my head and one for around my neck. I looked like mad Ophelia. Feeling completely ridiculous, *nil desperandum*, we set off for Hickstead. It was still broad daylight, and the two waiters, standing like sentinels either side of the wrought-iron garden gate armed with trays of glasses filled to the brim with champagne, made no attempt at hiding their surprise.

As if matters could be any worse, directly behind them was the French *équipe* elegantly attired in pressed chinos and dripping with cashmere. I wanted to die. 'Please don't tell us we are the only ones in fancy dress?' I asked. The waiters looked at each other and nodded.

Nightfall provided us with a merciful cloak. At around 11.00 p.m. the peace was disrupted by a noisy trio emerging from the house, dressed in purple: Lorna, Christopher Biggins and Elaine Paige. Elaine came over and confessed that she had once mistaken Dickie Davies (the ITV sports presenter) for Des Lynam. Before she could take a breath, convinced he was Graham Hill, she asked 'Tell me, Jimmy, what's the fastest you have ever driven?'

28

Hidden Talents

In February 1989 Bill Muddyman was due to spend the weekend with us and we suggested the Bunns came over for lunch. To make up the party we had also asked the Rt Hon Colin Moynihan MP, who was then Minister for Sport (now Lord Moynihan). Colin was flying solo, so Jimmy made a second phone call to Hickstead and the Bunns brought along a friend, Sally Ann Lasson, who delayed her return to London. All three pitched up after only a few hours' sleep. Jimmy suggested a bit of exercise would either kill or cure and, as it was exceptionally mild for the time of year, proposed a game of tennis.

Watching a struggling foursome from the sidelines, Lorna and Sally Ann mischievously whipped out a couple of condoms, pulled them over their heads and blew them up through their noses like balloons. Poor old Colin, who was about to serve, didn't know where to look. Unrepentant, the girls repeated their party trick during lunch. Colin wrote a couple of days later: 'I am still recovering from the tennis and look forward to a re-match! The lunch was delicious and the company has encouraged me to look again at my diary and see if I can come down to Hickstead. All the very best and once again my further thanks for a marvellous break in a perfect setting.'

I can't count how many dances and dinners Jimmy has taken me to over the last four decades or how many frocks I have worn. When I was skinny enough, I managed to wriggle into a couple of dresses made for my great-grandmother in India in the Thirties, but mostly I designed and made my own. In December 1989 we were due to attend the annual Christmas Ball given by SPARKS and, as usual, I was busy with needle and thread. Ma had passed on to me an antique black Brussels lace over-skirt, which had once again come from my great-grandmother's wardrobe. I wanted to show Jimmy how I was progressing with my latest venture into the world of couture, and so I slipped into the unfinished cherry red, strapless, boned dress, over which I placed the lace. I found him in the bath.

'Got any pins?' he asked, wiping soap from his eyes.

I gathered up the skirt and hobbled off to collect my sewing box. When I returned Jimmy was standing on the bathmat, stark naked and dripping wet. 'Hand me my glasses, turn around and stand still or I'll prick you.' Obediently, I didn't move a whisker while he tugged and tucked. 'There. Done,' he said, giving my bottom a pat. 'Stitch exactly where I've pinned; trust me.' I was astounded at Jimmy's hitherto hidden talent, but he explained that in the early years of his marriage to Gloria, he made all their curtains.

I wore the red dress (which hadn't cost a shilling over £15) to the SPARKS ball and sat next to HRH Prince Michael of Kent, whose wife, Princess Michael, is patron of the charity, and when the music started, the Prince asked me to dance.

We have dined with some of the best chefs in the business, from Gary Rhodes to the Roux brothers (Michel and Albert), and – last but not least – Monsieur Alain Ducasse. We first met Michel Roux Snr. at a gala dinner for the Duke of Edinburgh's Award Scheme. He was utterly charming and we got on like a house on fire. During the meal, the chap on my left asked me how long I had known Jimmy.

'Oh goodness, donkey's years,' I retorted, 'why?'

'Well, he hasn't taken his eyes off you all evening.'

We met Michel's brother Albert in the romantic setting of an exquisite bow-fronted house in St Catherine's Dock overlooking the Thames at Tower Bridge, the home of David Mellor and Penny, Countess Cobham. The traffic from Sussex to London had been dreadful and the journey took far longer than we anticipated. I had the beginnings of a throbbing headache, and when we sat down to eat I stared at the starter of squid salad. David and Penny are dear friends; I could not bear to upset them and cause a fuss, my embarrassment compounded by the fact that I was sitting next to our host. Wily Albert didn't miss a trick. 'Quick,' he said, 'no one's looking. Flip it onto my plate.' And with the sleight of hand worthy of a master prestidigitator, Monsieur Roux saved the day and I recovered in time for the main course.

My third culinary introduction was at a small gathering in the infamous Room 118 at the Cadogan Hotel, London. Previously the home of Lillie Langtry, it was where she used to entertain the future King Edward VII and where, in April 1895, Oscar Wilde was arrested for 'gross indecency'. We were guests of Monsieur Moro, the managing director of Lanson Champagne, and his wife, Marie-Laurence, who treated us to the very best of everything. I had the immense privilege of sitting next to Monsieur Ducasse, whose restaurant at the Dorchester has been awarded a well-deserved three Michelin stars.

Although we didn't have to sing for our supper, egged on by the atmosphere, food and wine, for some reason I was asked to propose a vote of thanks on behalf of all present – in French. Caught on the hop, the only thing that sprang to mind was a tongue twister, '*Un chasseur sachant chasser chasse sans son chien*'. Hardly appropriate after such a feast. Then, in a state of panic, I remembered, and recited, a childish French poem, 'J'ai bien mangé', written and recorded as a song by Patrick Topaloff in 1971.

29

'If music be the food of love ...'

I inherited my love of classical music from my father, but until I met Jimmy, opera was unknown territory apart from the 'Humming Chorus' from Puccini's *Madame Butterfly*, familiar through a *Music for Pleasure* LP record belonging to my parents. Jimmy encouraged me to appreciate this form of music by giving me tapes of highlights from the more popular works. He also taught me to love the mellifluous sounds of brass.

His mother's favourite aria was 'Mon coeur s'ouvre à ta voix' from *Samson and Delilah* by Saint-Saëns, which has since become my own cherished aria, the heart-breaking melody producing tears without fail.

'It wasn't that she had a wide knowledge of classical music,' Jimmy said in another radio interview with David Mellor, 'she was a very ordinary lady and it was simply that this piece of music stood out for her. I love the thrill of opera being sung so beautifully, the quality of the musicianship and the sound of the human voice.'

As we live only half an hour from Glyndebourne, for Jimmy's birthday in July I would endeavour to purchase returned tickets, and on our annual pilgrimage we have wept through *La bohème* twice, laughed through *The Marriage of Figaro* and been enchanted by *The Magic Flute*. One evening, the entire gamut of English eccentricity was in evidence. Rain had been falling heavily all day, and the temperatures had tumbled accordingly, making it impossible to picnic outside. When we arrived, Jimmy dropped me off under cover with the hamper and went off to park the car.

While I was waiting for him to return, an old Morris 1000 estate drove up and out stepped a middle-aged woman wearing a tatty Puffa coat over her long dress. 'Hurry up Gerald,' she boomed to her husband, adding, 'you'll find me where we always go.'

I didn't see 'Gerald' again, but was amused to notice that he, in an attempt to keep warm – along with many of the more senior opera buffs –sported what was obviously an old school pullover under his dinner jacket – one gentleman wore a pair of black rubber galoshes over his evening shoes.

Our tastes in music are catholic, and when we received an invitation to accompany Sir Desmond Pitcher (ex-chairman of Everton FC) and his wife Norma to see *The Rake's Progress* written in 1951 by Igor Stravinsky, with its iconic set designed by David Hockney, my blood turned cold. I had already seen the first Glyndebourne production in 1975 – as an extremely reluctant guest – and was dreading having to sit through it a second time. Sir Harry Secombe once admitted to Jimmy during the interval of a new musical that he hadn't heard a tune he could hum, and I feel the same way about 'modern' music – *The Rake's Progress* being a case in point.

The following year the generous Pitchers wanted us to return with them to the Sussex opera house and I had the cheek to ask which work we would be seeing. '*New Year*,' Desmond replied. A work by Sir Michael Tippett in three acts, it was commissioned by Houston Grand Opera, the BBC and Glyndebourne and was first performed in Texas in 1989. I had a pretty good idea of what to expect, and once again tried to persuade our friends that they might consider taking another couple who would appreciate its finer attributes.

Totally ignoring my pleas, they picked us up in plenty of time for us to imbibe a traditional Pimm's in the beautiful gardens by the ha-ha except, instead of lemonade as a mixer, Desmond asked the barman to use champagne. Jimmy studied his glass. 'Do you think, Des, if we added more champagne, will it make the Pimm's weaker?'

The first act was entitled 'The Space Ship Lands', and the tuneless jangling, hissing and other cacophonous noises emanating from the orchestra pit confirmed my worst fears. It was dreadful beyond words. We couldn't help but overhear some of the comments from the other opera lovers, who fell into two definite camps: those holding similar opinions to ours, and the intellectual brigade. Dreading further aural onslaught, we sank into our seats with the comforting knowledge that dinner would be waiting for us after the second act. Two down, one to go ...

We managed to stick it out and the journey home was interesting for two reasons: I gave Desmond's driver the wrong instructions when leaving the parking area and we turned left instead of right, and someone (who shall remain nameless) farted the whole way back to Hurstpierpoint.

At the end of November Jimmy received the news he had been dreading:

Buchan Hill died on Wednesday 28 November 1989, aged nearly 18, at the Kennels, Chipping Norton listening to the hounds he loved so much. He leaves one broken-hearted couple in Chastleton and doubtless another in Sussex. As the news of his passing becomes known many more will grieve, too. Instantly recognisable by his white markings he was probably the best-known horse in the Heythrop Country during the 14-odd years he hunted there. He had a heart as big as his head and was one of those rare equines, a true character and an absolute gentleman. His first, and what turned out to be his last, day of this season could not have been more enjoyable for him. Hounds unboxed here, and Buchan hacked on to the Meet with them. The sun shone, the 'going' was perfect and he was so well in himself that he allowed himself a buck. He hunted round his home village including Harcomb and Grove Farm, for some three hours, jumping a few fences and loving every minute. No one will ever know whether his leg was giving him trouble towards the end of the day because he was too proud and too brave a horse to do anything other than jog home absolutely sound. It was only when he got into the privacy of his own loose box that he admitted he was in any sort of discomfort. Buchan was loved by everyone who rode him or looked after him not only because he did everything – and more – that was asked of him but because he was such an incredibly rewarding friend. He liked people and they liked him. We are so proud, so lucky and so very, very grateful to have known him. He did one other thing. He started a friendship, which I hope will continue, despite his passing on.

133

Part Three
The Nineties – Naughty But Nice

30

Entente Cordiale

One afternoon at the All England Club while having a bath after a game of tennis, Jimmy overheard fellow member Sir Richard King mention a property for sale not far from his holiday home in the Dordogne in south-west France.

'I like the sound of that,' Jim interjected.

Jimmy didn't mess about and booked tickets for the ferry from Dover to Calais. The weather turned very nasty on the morning of our departure, and as our car crawled up the gangway towards the hold I felt a great deal of sympathy for Sydney Carton when being led to the scaffold. The wind was howling fit to bust and, combined with the terror of a choppy crossing mingled with the evil mix of ozone and engine oil, I felt queasy before we had loosened our moorings. We sought sanctuary in the warm, swirly-carpeted bar. Not feeling quite so chipper himself, Jimmy procured life savers in the form of two brandies mixed with double measures of Port while I watched with increasing trepidation as a steward deposited paper bags onto every surface.

'Is it going to be rough?' I asked him in a voice higher than normal.

Slap, slap, slap went the sick bags.

'Look at it this way, madam, you'll know you're on a boat.'

His prediction proved accurate and the storm whipped up to a force 8 gale; even some of the crew were ill. When we booked into a hotel that evening I phoned Ma to say we had arrived safely.

'Darling,' she announced, 'yours was the last boat out of Dover and they showed it on the six o'clock news!'

The next day we met up with the estate agent and, having seen the house, we made a tentative offer. He rang the owner only to be told that it had already been sold through another agent. The

November weather continued downcast and chilly, adding to our despondency. We were taken to see three further properties but, once again, we discovered none was available; we returned to England and empty-handed.

A few months later we decided to have another go, but in order to avoid disappointment, we did some research before we left. On St Valentine's Day 1990 we parked on rough grass in front of a 250-year-old stone property in the middle of farmland in the Lot-et-Garonne, a more rural department adjacent to the Dordogne. With the light fading and the electricity disconnected, we fumbled our way through the various rooms. In spite of stumbling over stacked boxes and odd pieces of furniture, and although there was damage (mostly cosmetic) from a burst pipe, the house was just about habitable. Having seen enough to tempt us, we put in an offer, which was accepted.

The papers were duly signed and, in possession of the keys, Ma and I flew out there in order to spring clean the place and raid the hypermarkets to equip it with new furniture, china, bedding etc.

The grass on the plot by now had grown to over 3 feet high and so we set about finding a willing victim to tidy up the garden. Our neighbouring farmers Daniel and Isabelle introduced us to a relation of theirs, Louis, a cheeky septuagenarian who looked as though he had emerged straight from Middle-earth. Not much taller as an adult than the undergrowth he was going to despatch, he had been deposited as a baby in a basket on the steps of the town hall in a nearby village and put up for adoption. He married for the first time in his sixties to a much younger girl, a happy union that produced a son. Louis couldn't get over how well I spoke French and each time we met told me the filthiest set of unrepeatable jokes I had heard in my life.

Jimmy loved it in *la France profonde*, delighted to be accepted at face value by our new friends who had little – or no – idea of his background. We tried to go as often as we could and, although his knowledge of French was limited, he did his level best to take part in conversations, which inevitably revolved around *'le foot'*. He relished the fact that he could wander about incognito – until we ventured into the Little England of the Dordogne, where a large

138

percentage of the inhabitants of Eymet in July and August seemed to be British. Anglo-Saxon voices uttering, 'Isn't that Jimmy Hill?' trailed us around every market square in the region and it became such a normal occurrence that I had a T-shirt printed for him with the words 'Yes it is' on the back, confirming their suspicions as their heads swivelled to follow us.

Our other neighbours, Monsieur and Madame Oden, who owned the farm to our left, were bewildered at the renewed invasion of Les Rosbifs, muttering that the Hundred Years War was far from over.

In late summer, having spent the night with friends in the Midlands, we were heading down the M1 on a Sunday morning to attend a SPARKS event in Luton when suddenly the traffic in front ground to a screeching halt. One or two people emerged from their cars to see what had occurred. We did the same and discovered that a few hundred yards in front a lorry containing frozen chickens had jackknifed, spilling its load across the three lanes. Luckily no one had been injured. Police cars and other recovery vehicles soon arrived on the scene but it became clear we were going nowhere. Then someone clocked Jimmy and asked for his autograph. I explained that we should be at a charity golf day for SPARKS and would it be cheeky to ask for a small donation in exchange? He was only too happy to comply.

Word spread and soon other travellers cottoned on, and with dozens of autographs 'sold', I couldn't hold the coins in my hands. A group of bikers, having propped their machines under a bridge, came looking for us and emptied their pockets of loose change. In the end we were stuck on the M1 for nearly three hours, during which time we had collected not only a few pennies short of £200 but also a bucket load of new friends now aware of the vital medical research carried out by SPARKS.

31

Third Time Lucky

In the early Eighties Jimmy recorded a programme for Radio 4 entitled *Be My Guest*, during which he chatted about his life, interspersed with his choice of music, including the song 'Makin' Whoopee', made famous in 1928 by Eddie Cantor. The lyrics told the story of a serial marrier who kept on having to come up before the judge when deciding the amount of alimony he should pay to the abandoned spouse. These irritations hit a particular chord with Jimmy and several of his male colleagues, many of whom had trodden the perilous bridal path not once, not twice, but sometimes, as in Jimmy's case, three times. I shall leave it to him to explain:

> I was member of a Luncheon Club, a group of reprobates from the world of football, writing and the theatre. Others included the likes of Brian Mears [past chairman of Chelsea FC], [Sir] Michael Parkinson, Bill Dodgin [team mate from Fulham], Michael Croft [director of the Shaw Theatre and founder of the National Youth Theatre of Great Britain], Willis Hall [playwright and author of *The Long, The Short and The Tall*] and Tom [Wilson]. We all led pressurised lives and would meet up in favourite haunts in order to eat, drink and sing. Clever American lyrics written in the Thirties were our choice of preference and we had a top ten of favourites. However, the club song was *Makin' Whoopee*, the subject of which is paying alimony. Now, would you believe, one or two members of the club have done a bit of this in their lives and so this song strikes a very bitter chord, may I say ... Fade to giggles and music.

> Perhaps they should have heeded the following words in the poem, *A word to Husbands*, written by Ogden Nash (1902–71):

Björn Borg and Jimmy, a very competitive duo

A cluster of stars gathered for the Goaldiggers: back row: Alan Weekes,
Brian Moore, Sir Elton John, David Wilkie. Front row: Dennis Waterman,
Jimmy, John Junkin and Eric Morecambe

Jimmy and Eric Morecambe – fun and games at the Goaldigger Ball

Jimmy, a brave and courageous horseman jumping for charity

Jimmy and Terry Wogan, friends off and on the course

With HRH Prince Philip and Telly 'Kojak' Savalas,
Ritz Club charity dinner

Our wedding day. Finally, after 15 years

A very proud day, collecting Jimmy's OBE
at Buckingham Palace © Rex Features

Lee Trevino, Jimmy, Peter Alliss, Ronnie Corbett and Seve Ballesteros,
a game of golf at St Andrews, thanks to the BBC
© Michael Joy

Jimmy, George and me at the Berkshire

HRH The Prince Edward, Jimmy and me at a fundraising dinner for the Duke of Edinburgh's Award Scheme

Desmond Lynam and Jimmy, two best mates

Opening the dance with HRH Princess Michael of Kent, Patron of SPARKS

Jimmy and Heather Mills McCartney. Jealous, moi?

Jimmy's last public appearance, and a fitting one, at the unveiling of a statue of him at the Ricoh Arena, Coventry City Football Club, July 2011

'To keep your marriage brimming
With love in the loving cup,
Whenever you're wrong, admit it,
Whenever you're right, shut up.'

I am not one to put a gun to someone's head and cry for an ulti-
matum and it didn't do my PR any good by bringing up the subject of
marriage. After fifteen years of living together eventually I gave up,
resigning myself to eternal spinsterhood.

On 1 December 1990 Jimmy and I made a trip to Reading for two
reasons: (1) Fulham were playing their rivals in the Third Division;
and (2) it was Roger Smee's last game as chairman of the Royals.
Roger's other half and Tom and Heather were booked in for the
night at the French Horn in Sonning, Berkshire, where we were all
having dinner together after the match. Reading won 1–0, a bad
result for Fulham which necessitated in a lot of fat chewing after the
final whistle blew.

Eventually we left the Madejski stadium and headed for the hotel
where we imbibed – or rather they did (I was on driving duty) –
more champagne. I am ashamed to say that, as the evening pro-
gressed and with the conversation limited to football, I became
increasingly bored and morphed into a proper Mrs Gruntfuttock.

Once back home I let George into the garden, and by the time I
went upstairs (still in my coat) Jimmy was in bed.

'I ... er ...' I stammered, 'I think I might go next door. I'll fidget
and you need your sleep. Busy day tomorrow.'

Giving a perfect imitation of Lady Bracknell he roared, 'What? I
have *never* been so insulted in my life!'

I was fagged out (it was now well past 2.00 a.m.). The only way
out of the situation was to cry, but blow me down, I couldn't
squeeze out a single teardrop. As a last resort I thought about when
Ulla was put to sleep.

'Right,' he said, smiling and taking my hand with one of his and
wiping away a tear with the other. 'Now Miss B, behave yourself. That's
sorted so give me a kiss.' Jimmy folded his arms across his chest, heaved
a sigh of relief and said, 'I have to say you looked so pretty in the car
driving home that I was considering asking for your hand in marriage.'

141

I was stunned. After three leap-year proposals (all turned down – he wasn't going to get a fourth; a girl does have her pride), I had finally got what I wanted.

'You'll have to take the whole package,' he rallied.

Hadn't I been doing that since we met?

'Now,' he persisted, 'will you marry me?'

On the morning of 2 December 1990 I wondered if it had all been a dream that I was about to become Mrs James Hill III.

'Do you remember anything about last night?' I asked, trying not to laugh.

No response from Jimmy.

'You can take it all back if you want,' I continued, 'I won't hold it against you. Promise.'

He walked over to the Aga, lifted the kettle and filled it with water. 'Of course I remember, silly thing. You're not accusing me of being drunk, are you?'

'Would I ever? What do you suggest we do now?'

'Ring Mama.'

Ma, at only six years his senior, shared a very tender relationship with Jimmy (referring to him as her sin-in-law before we were married), who happily included her in our plans, often ringing (when she was still in bed) saying that we were coming to pick her up in ten minutes, 'for an away day'. This generally meant pottering around antique shops before ending up in the pub or having fish and chips, cogitating over the *Telegraph* crossword.

Several times she joined us in France and on one occasion when we took the car, we stopped at a small hotel for the night. The proprietor led us upstairs and paused on the landing. 'This room is for the ... two people ...' she said, handing Jimmy a key and looking at him and Ma, 'and ... and this is for the single person,' looking at me. Ma laughed. 'Bad luck, James! Married to me again!'

When we sat down to supper there was a similar familial arrangement on the table next to us: Leo Abse (Welsh Member of Parliament and fervent campaigner for gay rights) was staying there with his wife and adult son. It is quite usual, as I discovered, for people in the public eye who haven't actually met to open up a conversation with each other. For example, in the infamous Eymet market one July day the actor Derek Nimmo (well known for his role in the Sixties television sitcom *All Gas and Gaiters*), on holiday in France with his wife, spotted Jimmy from across the square, came up to him and chatted, as though they had been lifelong friends.

That night, when Mr Abse realised with whom he was sharing the dining room, he said, 'How nice to see you, Jimmy, on holiday with your wife and daughter. Just like us.'

With Christmas in the offing, our thoughts turned away briefly from pending nuptials to the more important task of organising the house for the annual influx.

After breakfast on Christmas day Jimmy handed me a large package from under the tree. I unwrapped it carefully to discover that it contained a beautiful antique teapot. 'There's something else inside it,' he said. In the bottom was a sapphire and diamond ring.

Our engagement official, Jimmy consulted his diary and found that the first free day was 9 January but, because he was so busy, it was up to me to book the register office and pay for the special licence. I had waited so long for this moment that I wasn't going to start quibbling about who did what. Ma insisted that I wore something new and, with Jimmy working at the BBC, we rushed out and bought a cream, floaty dress in the sales. Unfortunately, I was larger than the lining, but we decided to buy it nevertheless. Before returning home, we nipped into M&S and bought an oyster satin nightdress which I cut it in half, stitched some elastic around the waist and created the perfect petticoat.

'Had a good day, girls?' Jimmy enquired, as Ma and I were knocking back our third tumbler of Amontillado. 'You'll never guess, Des asked if I was free to play golf with him next Wednesday. I said [because we were keeping it a secret] I couldn't and he kept on asking why.

Our wedding was only a whisker away. I didn't want a big fuss – lack of time prevented us from making elaborate plans anyway – and so only family no longer in short pants were invited. I didn't ask any of my old Knickers Grey friends (Uniform List: 6 pairs knickers white, 3 pairs knickers grey) from my Alma Mater, S Michaels Burton Park, Jimmy's excuse being that the house wasn't big enough and we would make too much noise. Ma bought a fruit cake from M&S that had been reduced in price, iced it, and decorated it with tiny footballers playing in front of a goalmouth she cleverly constructed from a piece of netting from a bag of oranges and a couple of toothpicks. The whole affair including frock, essential new underwear, cake, food, booze and a silver teapot as a special present from Ma to me came to well under five hundred smackers. In 2014 some bright spark carried out research (I wonder at whose expense?) proving that the cheaper the wedding, the longer the marriage lasted. QED.

On the eve of our official union Bill Muddyman invited Jimmy out for a Chinese in Esher to say farewell to his bachelorhood, along with Carole Chiswell-Jones (who was to be my witness), all of them coming back to stay the night in Sussex. The gang tumbled in noisily full of the joys at around half past eleven. Defying all traditions, and because we had a house full, I climbed into bed beside my groom to be.

The next morning (9-1-1991, an auspicious date if ever there was one) too excited, I was up with the birds and went to prepare breakfast for those brave and fit enough to face solid food. I jumped into a bath; five minutes later I extricated Jimmy from under the duvet, dumped him in my water while I got his clothes out (navy blue pinstripe suit – he chose the tie: the one embroidered with Father Christmases), and put on my glad rags.

With less than forty minutes to get to Haywards Heath, Ma arrived. 'This is for you to wear, darling. Nearly forgot: something blue.' It was the faded silk garter she had worn on her own wedding day to Dad in June 1948. 'Now for something old,' she said quietly, unfolding the antique lace veil treasured by generations.

In a flurry I kissed George goodbye and we left in Bill's Jaguar for the register office. There were no other guests apart from our witnesses, Ma, Carole and Duncan. It was my choice and perhaps a strange one, but I am not good at formal ceremonies (happy or sad) and I knew I would cry and didn't want to embarrass myself and everyone else so, as far as I was concerned, the smaller the gathering and the faster the deed was done the better. Needless to say, when it came to our vows, Jimmy and I were both in floods and totally incoherent. Gripping my hand tightly, he made three attempts to say my name in full, after which the registrar said, 'That will do Mr Hill. You may kiss the bride.'

Jimmy insisted that he wanted to whisk me off to the West Indies for our honeymoon, away from the January cold. I said that, what with the recession and with only a seven-day slot in his diary, the idea was lovely but not practical. It made much more sense to go somewhere nearer to home.

'What about Suffolk?' I suggested. 'Wobblywick [Walberswick]? Campsea Ashe? All log fires and cuddly? Pubs?' I pulled out my trump cards: 'Adnams beer, fish and chips?' (I always said that if I gave into Jimmy's daily request for this dish, it would kill him. Imagine the headline such an event would create: 'Jimmy Hill's wife batters him to death!')

'Would you really prefer Suffolk to Barbados?'

'Yes, actually, I would.'

'Ah', he said, flicking the paper. 'Fulham are away to Cambridge on Saturday. Okay, Suffolk it is then. You win.'

We were officially married by 10.00 a.m. on the Wednesday and the ink still wet as soon as we arrived home, I started cooking lunch. The roast beef went in the oven, Ma made the starter of prawns and melon, Mrs E buttered the bread and George clung to the Aga looking mystified. The house for the first time in ages was tidy and, with a blazing fire, flowers in every room and a banner over the fireplace saying, 'Eat, drink and remarry', I was a very happy bunny. Jimmy made a sweet speech and mid-afternoon, as it was starting to rain, we left for Pettistree. I drove us over the Dartford Crossing to the A12, heading for the old rectory where we had stayed once before with Ma.

The young couple recognised us instantly and, on seeing the bouquet I was carrying, smiled. 'Yes,' Jimmy confirmed, 'we were married this morning.' They quickly rustled up a chilled bottle of champagne and, after supper, we staggered upstairs to our old, familiar room. I went into the bathroom, leaving my new husband lying on the bed fully dressed. As I was squeezing toothpaste onto my brush I heard the television start up. 'Lovely,' I heard Jimmy say, '*Sportsnight.*'

We spent two happy days visiting my old haunts and discovering new ones together and, as I had promised, sampled the best local haddock cooked by two elderly ladies in Aldeburgh. Golf wasn't mentioned once, and neither was football until Saturday, which dawned, foggy, damp and perishingly cold. The approach to Cambridge was slow, complicated by a congested one-way system and, having circumnavigated the city twice, we eventually found the Abbey Stadium.

Pulling up alongside two policemen in front of large, solid double gates, Jimmy wound down his window. 'Could you point us in the direction of the directors' car park?' he asked. One of the officials confidently told us where to go and five minutes later we were driving through what looked like a public open space. Feeling something wasn't quite right, we carried on regardless, and passed under a low bridge before ending up in an area where there were dozens of coaches lined up side by side. We retraced our steps and, with renewed instructions, tried again, and failed.

The match had kicked off and, judging by the noise, a home goal had been scored. Like a scene from the film *Groundhog Day* we stopped for the third time by the two policemen. The younger of the two blushed, moved to one side and waved us through the gates behind him – into the directors' car park.

One afternoon several years later I called in at the chemist in Hurstpierpoint. There was a parking space outside the shop, albeit a bit on the tight side. I manoeuvred the car perfectly. Having locked it I glanced behind me and saw, standing at the window of the dry cleaners, Mr Sykes, the owner of the establishment, and Jim, our local traffic warden, both holding up placards giving me full tens for 'technical ability'.

The girls behind the counter in the pharmacy were laughing and one of them said, 'We've just heard this bloke on Radio 2 confessing that when he was a Special Constable on duty at Cambridge United he sent Jimmy Hill, who was on his honeymoon, three times around the city and, guess what? The poor man isn't a Special any more.'

For Jimmy, 26 June 1991 was an exciting day: a board meeting in the morning at Fulham, culminating with the 70th birthday celebrations for HRH Prince Philip in the grounds of Windsor Castle. We were the first to arrive, then Sir Michael Caine and his wife Shakira followed along with Sir Roger and Lady Moore. Shortly afterwards, the actor Simon MacCorkindale walked in with his wife Susan George. She and Jimmy had known each other from the past and, since both had a passion for horses, they had plenty to talk about.

Messrs Caine and Moore were joint Masters of Ceremony at the gala dinner in aid of the Duke of Edinburgh's Award Scheme, after which we enjoyed the most incredible firework display in the company of our host.

Don't ask me how or why, but I came across a dress for sale on eBay which had been worn at the party that night. Wonder what mine would have fetched?

32

Highs and Lows

At the beginning of the Fifties, Jimmy coached football at Butlin's holiday camp in Margate. Among the visitors was a group of young French students, one of whom, Jean Parquet, twelve or so years his junior, befriended Jimmy. Over the years they kept in touch, and Jimmy went to stay with him and his family in Brive-la-Gaillarde in France on the occasion of a wedding. They did meet up once again in Paris, but after that, for whatever reason, communications broke down.

Life throws up some extraordinary coincidences now and again and one day, among a bundle of correspondence forwarded by the BBC, was a letter with the words printed on the envelope '*Jean Parquet, Architecte, Brive*'. As it happened, our old farmhouse in the Lot-et-Garonne was only a couple of hours' drive away.

We couldn't believe it, hearing from Jean after more than fifty years. I phoned his office. Jean explained that he had recently received a group of English architecture students and, out of curiosity, asked if they had heard of a footballer called Jimmy Hill. 'Jimmy Hill?' they chorused. 'You mean *the* Jimmy Hill?'

When planning our next trip we contacted Jean and his wife Liliane, agreeing to meet them halfway at Les Eyzies-de-Tayac-Sireuil where, the two friends recognised each other instantly. During the meal an elegant, balding middle-aged man, a Kojak lookalike, came over to our table and enquired obsequiously if we were enjoying our lunch.

'That was nice of him,' I said. 'How charming. Is he the owner of the hotel?'

'*Non*,' Jean replied, stifling a chuckle in his napkin, 'he's an old colleague of mine. He's France's representative at the European Parliament in Brussels.'

In January 2015 Jean sent a card asking how we were, in particular how his old friend was faring. I rang straight away and Jean told me that he had recently written his own autobiography, *Une Vie Presque Ordinaire: Humeurs et Humour*. He sent me a copy and to my delight he had included a chapter on Jimmy, whom he described as being '*charismatique, et médiatique avant l'heure. Grand et athlétique. Mais il était tellement chaleureux qu'il dégageait un charme qui faisait fondre toutes les femmes*,' loosely translated as 'a mediator, ahead of his time. Tall and athletic, with so much charm and warmth that he melted women's hearts.'

We tried to go to France as often as Jimmy's diary allowed, and succeeded in six visits the first year, but our final trip in the summer of 1991 was tainted with anxiety. In 1976 he had undergone surgery for the removal of several benign polyps and we were worried they had returned. I felt that continuity of treatment was the best option and endeavoured to hunt down the surgeon who had carried out the original procedure.

After many telephone calls they located Jimmy's file on microfilm, only to be told that the surgeon had since retired. I managed to contact him and he suggested a colleague. An appointment was made the following week, and when I came to collect Jimmy after that first exploratory operation the nurse said Dr Zeegan wished to see me privately before we left for Sussex. Our conversation was brief.

'How long have you been married?'

'Nine months.'

'Oh, my dear, I am so sorry.'

'It's cancer, isn't it?'

That was about the only time the dreaded 'C' word was spoken out loud. Jimmy has already written about it, but I shall add a few lines if only to underline the immense courage he showed and the pragmatic way he handled this life-threatening illness. The surgeon wanted to operate straight away but Jimmy, professional to the end, insisted on waiting until after *Match of the Day* and, the programme over, on 12 September 1991 he caught a cab to the old Westminster Hospital in Horseferry Road and was admitted by the night staff.

After a tense five hours of surgery, Professor Wastell rang me to say that it had been a success. I caught the first train up to London. Luckily my mother had warned me in advance that Jimmy would be wired from every orifice, and I found him alive but not kicking. Although admitted under the National Health, because of his high profile, as soon as he was fit enough to leave the Intensive Care Unit, the Prof wangled a side room off the ward, where not only did Jimmy retain his sense of humour, but I never heard him once complain.

Des Lynam has always admired Jimmy's ability to confront problems head on. He told me:

Here are several instances of Jim being a real man: (1) When I was asked to present *Match of the Day* when it returned after a gap, I was worried about Jim's reaction, as he had been the main man for so long. With typical generosity he told me that if they had given it to anyone else he might have objected, but he told me he was happy for me to do it. (2) After I had had a memorable cock-up in Naples during the start of a world cup programme in 1990 I worried and fretted about it for days. Jim put an arm around me. 'Don't keep beating yourself up about it,' he said, 'remember the hundreds of great programmes you've done, not the one that got away.' (3) The wonderful sketches we did for Comic Relief: Jim, Hansen [Alan] and me in the *Blowing up of Jimmy Hill* and the *Why do we have to talk about football?* for Red Nose Day 2009. Both available on YouTube incidentally. He was brilliant in both. (4) His immense courage when he was suddenly taken ill during a cup final broadcast and went back to the programme as if nothing had happened. And finally, when he came and picked me up from the house after I had made a terrible mess of what should have been my private life. 'Not a day for being alone,' he said, 'you're coming with me. Bryony's got some soup on.' Jim is one of my heroes.

Sometimes I trundled along with Jimmy when *MOTD* was broadcasting live from a game, and 5 November 1991 was such an occasion when he had to be in Liverpool for the UEFA cup match against Auxerre (result: Liverpool won 3–0). We stayed with the rest of the

BBC team at the Atlantic Towers Hotel and the sole topic of conversation at breakfast the next morning was the shocking news of Robert Maxwell's unexplained death at sea, which remains a mystery even today. I tagged along to another match (probably linking the trip with some event we were expected to be at the following day); Des reckons it was most likely at Aston Villa.

It had been raining heavily all night and, on arrival at the ground, we were taken to the gantry only to discover that a few feet from Des and Jimmy's temporary desk, water was pouring through the roof into an old fire bucket. Des, when off camera during the transmission, put Jimmy on bucket-emptying duty.

As with most outside broadcasts, to curb costs there were no make-up girls, and I bought Jimmy a small powder compact and black mascara to cover the white on his moustache. Des started borrowing the powder and then so did everyone else on the *MOTD* team. In a lull in the proceedings I suggested to Des that the bucket would make a great close-up, and it did indeed get its moment of fame, with the world seeing what a dedicated lot they were.

Des told me of the day they were at Sheffield United to watch the game against Manchester United. It turned out to be a nightmare for the goalkeeper and, the match over, when Des and Jimmy were walking back around the pitch at Bramall Lane, they were approached by a good looking man dressed in a smart suit and tie.

'Good afternoon Mr Hill,' he said, 'did you enjoy the game?'

'Well,' Jimmy began, 'the goalkeeper came for it, totally missed it and . . .' Des jabbed him sharply in the ribs. 'He *is* the goalkeeper!' he whispered.

Quick as a flash, Jimmy turned things around, saying, 'But you weren't in any way to blame!'

When Des started to front *Match of the Day* Terry Venables became a regular pundit on the show, he and Jimmy rarely sharing the same point of view. They often ended up having a heated argument – perfect television viewing. Terry said that whenever he climbed into the back of a black cab, almost without fail, every driver asked the same question.

'You really 'ate that Jimmy Hill, don't you?'

'No, we get on fine.'

'Go on, you *really* 'ate him!'

'No,' said Tel, 'I don't.'

'Yes, you do.'

'No.'

'You can tell me. Yeah, you 'ate him.'

'You're right. I hate him.'

Terry told me:

I have to admit that there are many fond memories of working with Jimmy but one of my favourite moments is when we were on *Match of the Day* on a Saturday night when it was that time of the year when everyone had to put their clocks back an hour. After all the reviews of the football matches and the show was coming to an end, Jimmy sat up straight, looked into the camera and said, 'Don't forget, after this wonderful show, you must have a nice cup of cocoa and, whatever happens, this is the one night of the year you must not forget to put your cocks back.' This programme was live and millions of people were given these words of wisdom. Jimmy was oblivious of his trip up until he saw me and the camera crew laughing; realising his faux pas, he said, 'Sorry about that!' Jimmy said afterwards that he would have been absolutely fine to the bitter end until Barry Davies sniggered and he heard (through his earpiece) the producer saying, 'Don't be a bloody fool Barry, it could happen to you sometime.'

I have toured the United Kingdom from Ullapool (Johnny Haynes bet us, in Harry's Bar in Edinburgh, that we would not travel so far north – we did) to the Cornish toe because of either Jimmy's charity obligations, the BBC or, more often than not, his responsibilities as director/chairman of a football club. Thus I have visited Grimsby, Doncaster, Macclesfield, Chesterfield, Wrexham – you name it, I've been there, done it, got the T-shirt. A weekend before Christmas not long after we were married I was subjected to end-to-end football, starting off with a game at Coventry on the Saturday afternoon.

Having managed to inveigle Jimmy from the cushioned comfort of the boardroom, I drove us across to Blackpool, where Charlton (or was it Fulham?) were due to play the following day. Arriving at the motorway hotel in time for dinner, I was feeling distinctly off colour and, troubled by sore glands in my neck, I barely slept a wink all night. As dawn broke I went into the bathroom and, under the unforgiving strip light, noticed that my jawline was bigger than when I went to bed. I woke Jimmy.

'You'll do anything to get out of watching a match,' he said jokingly, 'but you're right, your face is a bit puffy.'

Concerned, he went to reception, where they summoned the doctor.

'And how old is your wife, Mr Hill?' the medic asked, none too pleased at having his Sunday lie-in cancelled.

'Forty-one? Forty-two?'

'And she thinks she has mumps, does she now?' He sat on the bed and palpated my neck. 'Your wife has mumps.'

I know things have changed considerably since those early days when, as a director, Jimmy would go into the boardroom while I mingled with the other wives in the Ladies' Room. Most of the time they were all dyed-in-the-wool fanatics and talked non-stop about the game, the players, the results and so on, all of which passed straight over my head. Feeling isolated and lonely, I found comfort in hot tea and food. It was no different when I went to watch home games at either Charlton or Fulham and, although I knew the other directors' wives, I couldn't enter into a conversation, my lack of knowledge nobody's fault but my own.

One very cold Tuesday night Jimmy asked me to go with him to Charlton, who were still playing at the Valley before they had to move on a temporary basis, ground-sharing with Crystal Palace. 'I won't stay long afterwards and we'll nip out for a Chinese,' Jimmy promised. I was dispatched to the Ladies' Room and, because we were eating later, I avoided the nibbles. Silly me. Everyone else went home, the cleaner came in, vacuumed crumbs from the carpet and turned off most of the lights. The door opened.

'We had to have an emergency board meeting. Did you have any of those garlic prawns?'

'What prawns?'

'. . . Steak and kidney pudding?'

The Chinese definitely off the menu, as we hurtled through the Rotherhithe Tunnel I was feeling increasingly bolshy, and asked why on earth he made me go to the games since we were only together during the match itself. He prised my hand off the gear stick and squeezed it.

'I ask you to come with me because I like to know you're there,' he said, echoing the words of A. A. Milne:

> Piglet sidled up to Pooh from behind. 'Pooh?' he whispered.
> 'Yes, Piglet.'
> 'Nothing,' said Piglet, taking Pooh's hand. 'I just wanted to be sure of you.'

Jimmy loves a bargain, and away fixtures provided the opportunity to indulge in his other favourite hobby: shopping. The highlight in Hartlepool on New Year's Day was a trip to B&Q where we purchased three beach towels bearing the insignia of Manchester United, lured by the fact that they were only a quid each. Another weekend Charlton were due to play Torquay and once again we were billeted with the team. With time to kill before kick-off, we travelled to the pretty coastal town of Dawlish, bought some cider and clotted cream, and when Jimmy spotted the large 'sale' sign on a shoe shop, ten minutes later he walked out with a new pair of brogues.

Jimmy adored dancing, was always hot to trot and could strut for England. I didn't and still don't, apart from a few granny moves behind closed doors; in public I become stiffer than a broom handle. In February 1992 the University of Aberdeen invited him to speak at its ball where, after a few anecdotes, the audience was entranced. The speech over, the ceilidh started and Jimmy was whisked onto the dance floor by a bevy of highland beauties. Feeling more than a touch wallflower-ish and fully aware, with the best will in the world, that I had temporarily lost my other half, I stayed as long as politeness allowed. Morpheus won the battle and I retired discreetly to our room, leaving Jimmy in the thick of it. Fuelled by an endless stream of amber nectar, he bopped and hopped until light stopped play.

In the spring of 1991, we travelled to Kenya to take part in a golf competition to raise money to build fenced enclosures to protect the rhinos. We were to stay at the Windsor Golf and Country Club outside Nairobi, a magnificent colonial-style residence that had recently opened. In the tournament I was teamed up with Donna Hurt (the actor Sir John Hurt's ex-wife), who was living in their old marital home in the hills, and, both novices, we proudly completed the course in regulation 36. As a result, the club professional presented me with my official handicap certificate.

We had become friendly with an ex-pat English couple and they invited us to play golf with them on Sunday at the exclusive Muthaiga Golf and Country Club, followed by lunch. The club featured in the 1987 film *White Mischief*, with Charles Dance and Greta Scacchi in the starring roles (the latter used to live in our village until recently). Having completed the round, we went to shower and change before having a drink in the cool, colonnaded atrium; it was like a step back in time. After more *burra-pegs*, the wife suggested that it was high time we should go in to eat, but contrarily her husband ordered another round. She became fidgety and, with no further argument to put forward, he acquiesced.

No sooner had we sat at our table than a couple approached us.

'Fancy seeing you here, Jimmy!' the wife chirruped. 'You won't remember, but we last met up in the Isle of Man.'

Pleasantries over, they departed, leaving our male companion very pink around the gills. Like a scene from the film, his other half leapt out of her chair like a scalded cat, nodding urgently in the direction of the cloakroom.

Lights, camera: ACTION!

'It's perfectly awful!' the poor thing sobbed. 'That *person* is my husband's mistress!'

CUT!

After the tournament we were treated to a few nights at the Siana Springs safari camp in the Maasai Mara, which meant catching another plane. I am a very nervous flyer at the best of times and, having flown in the tail end of a swaying, ancient Dakota, enquired apprehensively as to what sort of craft awaited us. They reassured me it was nothing at all to worry about. At the airport we were taken to a small building and, after the necessary formalities, walked out onto the tarmac where we were confronted by a tiny yellow contraption hung together by a wing and a prayer, not much bigger than a garden swing seat and clearly not in the first flush of youth.

'Has our plane been delayed?' I asked, white-knuckled.

'Nope,' came the succinct reply.

A Scottish father and son, both well over six feet tall, strode behind us onto the runway. With no visible means of access, the Asian pilot plonked his hands on my backside and, after the count of three, shoved me up onto the wing. I scrambled inside. *Père et fils* followed, folded their long legs and squeezed into the rear two seats. Jimmy was last on board and sat beside our captain at the front: a two-one-two formation. As we prepared for take-off, Jimmy mentioned that his door (the window 'attached' with vulcanised tape) was still wide open, only to be advised, 'Wait until we're up in the air and then give it a good bang.'

At the mercy of the thermals, the more we climbed, the more turbulent it became. 'Dad,' the son groaned less than 18 inches behind me, as we hit yet another air pocket, his breath hot on my neck, 'I wish we hadn't had that curry in Nairobi.'

Not a minute too soon, with mutual relief we deposited them in one piece at Governor's Camp. We heard through the grapevine that they were unable to check in straight away as a young and extremely bumptious bull elephant had wandered into reception and was disrupting things by tossing everyone's luggage into the air before trampling on it.

The remainder of the flight at a lower altitude was compelling and, flying only a few hundred feet above wild animals familiar from television or magazines, my earlier fears vanished. Forty minutes later, after a safe if somewhat cavalier landing, we were driven by Land Rover for a further twenty minutes across unmade roads pitted with hazardous potholes.

With no perimeter fencing, the camp was open to scrubby bush and the world beyond, our tent pitched at the outer limits. Jimmy, who is not a good traveller, wanted to lie down, whereas I picked up my camera and went walkabout. Fifty yards away from our tent I stumbled upon a family of warthogs; I don't know who was more startled. On spotting me, the mother turned on her stilettoes and trotted off, her striped young in single file behind, their whippy tails waving in the air like radio antennae. At supper I was severely admonished by the warden, who said my stupid behaviour could have resulted in me being eaten by a lion or charged by a wildebeest.

Talking of lions, it was a strange experience being in the middle of the wilderness with only a millimetre or two of canvas separating us from the claws and jaws of deadly predators. I did a little research before our departure and read an article on safaris which appeared in one of the Sunday papers. The female journalist, an African virgin like me, described a series of bloodcurdling screams and grunts which disturbed her sleep during the night. Imagining some poor creature was being devoured alive, she mentioned it at breakfast, only to be told (accompanied by hoots of laughter) that the noise was caused by a honeymooning couple in the adjacent tent.

In January 1993, having celebrated our second wedding anniversary, we had the idea to invite Terry Venables and Bobby Moore to lunch. Both of them, like Jimmy, had recently become legally bound to their much younger long-term girlfriends: Terry had married Toots (Yvette), Bobby had married Stephanie and, of course, Jimmy had finally grasped the business end of a stinging nettle and married me, the consensus being that all three gentlemen felt they were getting on a bit.

Jimmy and Bobby were old sparring partners, both having enjoyed playing for Fulham. David Mellor, when he was interviewing Jimmy for *Across the Threshold* on Classic FM in October 1998, put forward the sad truth that many who had achieved great heights in their field floundered and threw it all away, citing George Best (another ex-Fulham player) as a prime example. Jimmy spoke about the day when the Goaldiggers organised a football match at Walton and Hersham, in which George, having retired from the professional game, was taking part. Jimmy recalls:

I gave the ball to him, he went past several people, and destroyed the opposition. He had learned to cope with age and the frailties of his body, played the ball quite beautifully and went looking for the opposition to beat. I turned round to speak to Bobby [Moore] who was playing alongside me and said, 'you know Bob, that's why he's so different, isn't it? We ran away [from the opposition] and he goes to them.'

Our table seats eight, so we asked Des, thinking he might be prodded into following suit and marrying Rose, but when he got wind of the reason behind the invitation, jokingly denied he had 'reached that stage'. Sadly, before we could fix a mutually convenient date for the get together, barely a month later in February poor Bobby tragically succumbed to bowel cancer. It would have been a good lunch. Rose and Des are perhaps two of our closest friends and I am so pleased to report that they are now married. For several years they spent Christmas with us, along with their beloved Westie Daisy. What happy days they were.

33

Hissy Fits

If you can keep your head when all about you
Are losing theirs and blaming it on you,
If you can trust yourself when all men doubt you,
But make allowance for their doubting too;
If you can wait and not be tired by waiting,
Or being lied about, don't deal in lies,
Or being hated, don't give way to hating
And yet don't look too good, nor talk too wise.'

—from Rudyard Kipling, *If*

Jimmy never shied away from speaking his mind. In an interview with Steve Allan for *Sun Sport* on 25 March 1977, Richard Dinnis [caretaker manager of Newcastle United] lashed out at Jimmy's comment on air after the match:

> Jimmy Hill should take a look at his own team before pontificating on TV about a physical approach to football. Charity begins at home.

Jimmy replied to Mr Dinnis four days later:

> After a lifetime in football I have come to realise that it serves no useful purpose for those of us involved in any capacity with clubs to be seen squabbling through the columns of newspapers. I trust you believe in fair play as I do and, if so, would ask whether on reflection you might feel you have been unfair to yourself, to the BBC in particular, and also to me. I did not see the match and tackles you referred to in *The Sun* and thus had no opportunity to condemn Coventry players for their

behaviour. In my role as analyst and BBC presenter I have condemned vicious conduct whatever the player or club and with the BBC's backing will continue to do so.

History repeated itself when on 30 January 1994 the BBC was at Carrow Road to broadcast the live match between Norwich City and Manchester United. There was a right old hoo-ha during the first 45 minutes and a second after half-time. Jimmy, who saw the incidents unfold, commented in his inimitable way. This did not go down at all well with the then Mr Ferguson.

The following appeared in the *Daily Telegraph*:

Ferguson reacted angrily when told Hill had been severely critical of Eric Cantona who made a reckless, lunging challenge on Jeremy Goss in the first half and kicked John Polston on the head 17 minutes from time. Hill described Cantona's actions as 'despicable' but Ferguson retorted: 'Jimmy Hill is verbal whenever it suits him. I'm not interested in Jimmy Hill, neither are my players. He writes us off in the warm up – that's how much he knows about the game.'

During the post-match interview Sir Alex declared Jimmy a 'prat' in front of millions of viewers. In the *Daily Mail* on 1 February he was quoted as saying, 'I was incensed at him using words like "villainous and despicable".'

Four days later, on 3 February, Sir Alex wrote to Jimmy recognising the impact of his knee-jerk reaction:

I am writing this letter with the most sincere apologies for my unwarranted attack on you last Sunday at Norwich. I have always maintained that there is nothing wrong with losing one's temper so long as it is for the right reasons, but on this occasion there was no valid reason.

Jimmy responded with equal respect:

Thank you very much for your letter, which I was very pleased to receive. Believe me, I understand only too well the pressure on a manager, especially just after a game, to protect his players. As I'm sure you will realise, I have to speak out too for other reasons. I can't wait for the opportunity to share another dram or two so that we can sympathise with each other's problems. Meantime, keep up the good work!

By fair means or foul Manchester United beat Norwich City 2-0.

On 27 April 1994 the *Daily Telegraph* printed an article called 'A Bit of Larkin About', written by someone using the pseudonym 'Fantasist'. The article begins: 'The *Fantasy League* has its first poet laureate. He's called Larkin. Steve Larkin. The poem's called *Sick as a Parrot Over the Moon* and, as you can see it's a coruscating lampoon on the football pundit's penchant for clichés, "especially Jimmy Hill".'

Jimmy penned his own verse:

Listen young whippersnapper - try rhyming with that!
This is an ode from a passionate prat.
I'm flattered indeed to be your Number One
But why in *The Telegraph* and not in *The Sun?*
Such illustrious readers understand grammar
And would rather not have me put under the hammer.
Could it just be that I criticised Eric
Thus falling from grace like a criminal cleric?
When it comes down to clichés I'm hardly a runner,
Though I won't blast my colleagues - not even a Gunner.
So make with your metaphors, be careful of tense
And don't let your loyalties make rhyming non-sense!

34

The Order of the British Empire

*Not that I haven't achieved anything - I have - but I've never ingratiated
myself to the Establishment to the extent that I would be publicly rewarded.*
—Jimmy Hill, *c.*1972

On 14 November 1994 a registered letter arrived from 10 Downing
Street:

> The Prime Minister [the Rt Hon John Major MP] has asked me to
> inform you, in strict confidence, that he has it in mind, on the
> occasion of the forthcoming list of New Year Honours, to sub-
> mit your name to The Queen with a recommendation that Her
> Majesty may be graciously pleased to approve that you be
> appointed an Officer of the Order of the British Empire.

I was thrilled and very, very proud. Mrs Edwards (our housekeeper)
composed this poem in celebration:

Prince Philip said to Lillibet
'In nineteen ninety-five my pet
Forgive my pointing out to you,
Some decoration's overdue.'
'You don't suggest,' she cried with heat,
'The throne room needs re-gilded seat?
Or that the ceiling in the loo
Could use some paint from B&Q?'
'No, no!' he said, 'They're far from goners ...
I speak, my love, of New Year's Honours.
There's one I've watched, full many a year

From when, hirsute from ear to ear
He filled the screens of half the nation,
Wise judgement gave, or commendation.
From wide and past experience spake,
And rose above each Mickey take,
Made every point with clarity
And faced close shaves for charity.'
'I can't imagine who you mean . . .
Pray tell me more,' replied the Queen.
'Not in . . .' her voice rose to a scream,
'Our *horribilis* cricket team?'
'No, no,' he soothed, 'Perish the thought.
Try all the other forms of sport.
With soccer, tennis, golf and all
He's known for being on the ball.
Fund-raising auctions? He's a must,
And does much for the Prince's Trust.'
'Of course,' she cried, 'Don't tell me, Phil
It's one James William Thomas Hill.
And yes, you're right, I shall decree
The latest score's an OBE.'

Telegrams came in thick and fast from the top brass at the BBC, Buckingham Palace and the world of football. Lt-Gen Sir James Wilson (football correspondent for the *Sunday Times*) wrote this charming letter summing up everyone's delight:

James, very many congratulations on your award of the OBE in the New Year Honours. Your many friends will be delighted not because they know how many times over it has been earned and deserved. You have made an exceptional contribution to football. First of all in the way you played – I have such happy memories of you at Brentford and Fulham. You enjoyed the game, played it well, and won or lost with grace and dignity. Johnny Haynes, a great player, owes much to your example, and to your ability to see the game in perspective. Next, you got the players properly rewarded. It was a great battle; you fought it firmly, correctly and with humour. Soon afterwards at Coventry you showed how to manage in the changed circumstances. Subsequently, as a commentator, you explained the game not only to ordinary people but to those who thought, wrongly, they understood it! And thirdly, you stood up for referees and interpreted their problems. But all this was just the tip of the iceberg. Your services to the world as a whole and the Boys' Club movement in particular, has been outstanding. Well done indeed. I have been lucky to count you as a friend.

A knock-on effect was that in February 1995 Jimmy was the subject of *This is Your Life*. It was a wonderfully heart-warming programme, and the sports journalist Giles Smith showed his enthusiasm in an article he wrote for the *Independent*:

What a turn-around this was. It wouldn't even be fair to say that Jimmy Hill slotted into that possibly mythical category – the people you love to hate. More often than not, hating Jimmy Hill has involved having a really bad time. But from now on, at every point at which one is tempted to turn rancorously against him, one will be haunted by a sequence from Wednesday night's show in which Hill, handed a cornet by one of a cheerful bunch of his old marching-band pals, promptly delivered a quick burst of the '*Eton Boating Song*', pausing with perfect comic timing before nailing the high note at the end. At home, blinking away the tears, one was forced to confront the utterly unthinkable: Jimmy Hill in 'Really Nice Man' Shock.

In March we returned to Africa, this time to Zimbabwe on behalf of Help the Aged. The country, then known as the food basket of Africa, was a wonderful place with a thriving, rich agriculture. However, on the other side of the coin much was needed to improve the lives of those less privileged. Robert Powell and his wife Babs (one of the original Pan's People dance troupe), Tim and Christine Brooke-Taylor, and Dave Woolf (a Mancunian comedian) and his wife Alice made up the party, along with our old pal and pack Akela, Jerry Stevens.

We stayed a couple of nights in a private estate in Harare where we each had our own thatched cottage near the tennis court and swimming pool. Thoroughly spoilt and pampered, we were brought swiftly back to reality when we visited one of the villages, the reason for our trip. The dozens of celebrities who take part in charity tournaments are regularly presented with goody bags, which often contain a pullover, many of which never get worn. Therefore, a few weeks before the trip, Jerry asked us to donate as many of these jumpers as we could. Even though the climate is temperate in Zimbabwe it can get cold at night and the sweaters would provide welcome warmth to those less fortunate Africans.

The climax was a gala dinner given at the Leopard Rock Hotel, a four-hour drive away in the Bvumba Mountains in the Eastern Highlands. When the Queen Mother stayed there in 1953 she declared it the most beautiful part of the African continent she had ever visited. During the bush wars of the Seventies, it was severely damaged by rocket fire and subsequently closed until 1980 when, following total refurbishment and the installation of an 18-hole championship golf course, it was re-opened with every creature comfort imaginable. Built along the lines of a French château, with the exterior stucco painted sugar mouse pink, it is a true fairytale palace. We were given the Presidential suite (next to the turret room where the Queen Mother had slept) and it was a very strange feeling being in the same super-king-sized bed as President Mugabe – but thankfully not at the same time.

If there was ever a shortfall at a SPARKS golf day I was sometimes called upon to fill the gap. A particular favourite (in which I took part in an official capacity) was the last tournament of the season held at the Addington in Shirley, near Croydon. It was a challenging course at the best of times, and we felt honoured when we were invited to become members of this old-school, traditional club.

Jimmy was also a member of the Berkshire Golf Club, renowned for its Sunday lunches. To sit down to one of Sam (an Aldershot supporter) the Chef's roasts was my reward for waking at dawn in order to de-ice the windscreen and get Jimmy out of bed and into the car so that he was on the tee at 8.30 a.m.

Puddings were yummy, my favourite a combo of baked rice with loads of skin and a substantial dollop of steamed syrup sponge. One Sunday I couldn't decide whether to add cream or custard so, casting all cares to the wind, I poured on both. As I was about to return to our table, one of the elderly waitresses sped up the aisle and banged into me by mistake, resulting in my plate chucking its entire contents down the back of the girl in front of me. Dressed from head to toe in cashmere (wouldn't she just?) she was, naturally, very upset. I, too, was mortified by such a display of clumsiness and returned shame-faced to our table empty-handed. Five minutes later Jimmy encouraged me to try again. 'Quick!' he said. 'Off you go while there's no one there.' I stood up and started to walk across the dining room, only to hear him shout, 'Fore!'

35

A Man with Many Strings to His Bow

Some years ago, Jimmy was made the third Life President of SPARKS, following in the footsteps of Leonard Cheshire (Group Captain the Lord Cheshire VC OM DSO DFC) and R. E. 'Buzzer' Hadingham OBE CBE (Chairman of the All England Lawn Tennis & Croquet Club, 1984-89). Buzzer, a keen writer of what he referred to as 'doggerel', wrote a tribute to Jimmy, which he read out at a SPARKS dinner in January 1996:

Way back in 1960
Duncan Guthrie had a thought
He sought the help of famous stars
Outstanding men of sport.
He argued most persuasively
It really would be apt
To work to raise essential funds
To help the handicapped.
Wally Barnes was one of four
And Jimmy Hill another
Jim Laker too was counted in
Dai Rees became the other.
From modest start this famous four
Collected without cease
At every type of sports event
They watched the funds increase.
Alas, the Reaper's fatal scythe
Cut down Wally, Dai and Jim
Thus leaving one of four with us
We still rejoice in him.

Dear Jimmy Hill we all salute
Your talent to inspire
We thank you for your leadership
Your energy and fire.
But if you think you now can sit
At ease to sleep or dream
No way, old friend, you still remain
Our auctioneer supreme.
For all you've done we thank you now
You really have been great
There's one request we leave with you,
Just keep on helping, mate!

It was customary for Jimmy to lead Buzzer's Canadian wife Lois onto the dance floor while I would have a shuffle with her husband. As I made a desperate attempt to keep up with my partner's energetic footwork, Jimmy and Lois sashayed elegantly past. With a look of complete understanding on her face, I heard Lois explain to Jimmy, 'Buzz did tap.'

Jimmy was always a willing part of the team and appeared on countless light entertainment programmes, including *The Mrs Merton Show*. After the broadcast Lisa Mayhew (the assistant producer) wrote to Jimmy: 'You were a brilliant guest and you are also a thoroughly nice man!' Caroline Aherne, aka Mrs Merton, added her own PS: 'Jimmy – you were great and I love you! Caroline X'.

In November 1996, he took part in *An Evening with Bruce Forsyth*, where he was pulled out of the audience to perform off the cuff with the great man himself, along with Sir Matthew Pinsent (Olympic gold medallist) and Ian Wright (Arsenal, England). With no prior warning or rehearsal they did a pretty good top hat and cane routine. Bruce wrote:

Many, many thanks for allowing me to use you in the TV show. The more years I do audience participation, makes me even more grateful to the people who get up from their seats and have a go at anything. I just wanted to let you know that I do appreciate it and hope you will be pleased with your ad-lib performance. PS At last we've done our act on TV.

The 'act' to which Bruce was referring was when they put their two famous chins together and raised them like Tower Bridge.

Jimmy took great pride in writing the words to two club songs – one for Arsenal and, along with John Camkin (journalist and sports administrator), the other for Coventry City. These are the opening lyrics of 'Good Old Arsenal', sung to the tune of Rule Britannia: 'Good old Arsenal / We're proud to sing that name / And while we sing this song / We'll win the game.'

'The Sky Blues Song' is sung to the tune of the Eton Boating Song. These are the updated lyrics: 'Let's all sing together, / Play up Sky Blues, / While we sing together, / We will never lose. / Proud Posh or Cobblers, / Oysters or anyone / They can't defeat us, / We'll fight till the game is won.'

He also wrote these words to be sung to the tune of 'Wouldn't It Be Lovely', from *My Fair Lady*:

All we want is a pitch somewhere
A ball that's round and a ref that's square
To play without a care,
Oh, wouldn't it be lovely?
Lots of goals from the forwards' feet
Lots of scoreboards that say, 'clean sheet'
Add up to victor sweet
Oh, wouldn't it be lovely.
Oh, so lovely dribbling down the field to score a goal
And when Kevin shoots it's always
Right in that little 'ole
Skipper Em' says they should not pass
If they do they'll end up on the ... grass
Did I say grass? What farce!
Oh, wouldn't it be lovely, lovely ... lovely.

Another famous football song, 'Three Lions', music by Ian Broudie, words by David Baddiel and Frank Skinner, was to be the Official England Song for Euro '96. Jimmy bumped into the boys one afternoon, having finished an interview on the radio. I shall leave it to Frank to describe what happened, as recounted in his auto-biography *Frank Skinner by Frank Skinner*:

> We sang the song at the BBC *Sports Review of the Year* for 1996. Dave and me turned up for the rehearsal in the afternoon and then we had time to kill before the real event that evening, so Jimmy Hill, a man we had both watched on the telly since we were kids, invited us back to his hotel room. We ordered chips on room service, took our shoes off, and all three of us sat up on Jimmy's bed with our plates on our laps and watched Chelsea versus Southampton on Sky, with Jimmy doing analysis and expert comment throughout.

One sunny day Jimmy received an advance from his publisher and we decided to drive to Brighton for a breath of sea air. Without warning he dived off the road into a car showroom and, half an hour later, he was the proud owner of a bright red Alfa Romeo. Some weeks later at about 2.30 in the morning when I was behind the wheel after having spent the evening with some friends, we were stopped at the junction of the A23 and the A272 by a man in uniform waving a torch who, we could see, was laughing.

'Sorry,' he said, struggling to control himself, 'have you been drinking, madam?'

'No, I haven't. Well, not for a couple of hours at least.'

'Then I must apologise for my behaviour. It's just that the last car we pulled over was being driven by a 6′4″ transvestite in a red frock and black fishnet stockings.'

'Shine your torch onto the man sitting next to me.'

'Oh, it's you Jim. What a night! You only live down the road. Off you go.'

Jimmy has a brilliant analytical brain and, had he not chosen a sporting career, he would have made an excellent lawyer and I have heard him put forward an argument – equally successfully – from both sides of the fence. He was called upon by the Football League to be chief witness following a nasty tackle on a player which ended his career. A video of the incident was sent through and Jimmy studied it at close quarters, checking and verifying every kick and lunge in preparation for the hearing. Jimmy caught the train to London, and Gordon McKeag (chairman of the Football League) was in charge of proceedings. Afterwards he and his wife gave Jimmy a lift back to Sussex, where they were to have dinner with us and stay the night.

When we were in the middle of the main course Gordon asked me, 'What would it mean to you if I said *Ready, Steady, Cook?*'

'Jimmy went on it once,' I replied.

'Well, when he was in the middle of giving his evidence at the hearing, the crucial part of the tape stopped and in its place was Ainsley Harriott.'

36

Near Misses

On 3 April 1997 Jimmy and I travelled back to Liverpool to watch the Grand National. This was my first visit to Aintree but Jimmy had been there many times before, once in 1975 to perform a publicity stunt for *Sportswide*, the weekly sports magazine for the daily early evening programme *Nationwide*, the day before the big race itself. Knowing that he could ride, the BBC thought it would be a great promotion for Saturday's *Grandstand* if they could persuade him to jump the first fence on the notorious circuit. Having hunted over some fearsome country, Jimmy accepted.

In an interview with Brian Radford for *The Sporting Life* (23 February 1979) Jimmy said, 'I'm usually game for anything, so I asked Terry Biddlecombe [champion National Hunt jockey who had ridden for HM The Queen Mother] to join me.' Before they climbed in the saddle Terry whisked Jimmy away for a heart starter in the form of a stiff tot of whisky – a gesture which frightened him to death.

'What if the horse decides he wants to carry on and I can't stop him?' Jimmy asked anxiously.

'Jump the first,' Mr Biddlecombe replied, 'jump the second, but for fuck's sake, don't jump the third!'

Things turned out very differently for us on that beautiful spring day in 1997 which had started out so well, just months before Princess Diana died in August. Once again we were guests of the BBC, and Jimmy suggested we check out the runners and riders in the paddock before placing our bets for the 3.45 p.m. race, time spent on research and all that. Having grabbed our coats, we worked our way through the crowd and rubbed camel-clad shoulders with Gregory Peck (still handsome at 81), then spotted Des Lynam in the middle of a live interview with Jenny Pitman.

The euphoric festive atmosphere suddenly shattered. Sirens sounded and orders were barked from every loudspeaker, telling us to leave the immediate area on foot, adding that all the car parks were out of bounds. Imprisoned, within the concourse and surrounded by thousands of equally confused faces, we were forced to follow the seething mass away from the paddock onto the racetrack.

I remember walking past the legendary jumps, which towered above our heads, dwarfing us completely. A group of exuberant young men, no doubt spurred on by the intoxicating combination of alcohol and adrenalin, and clearly oblivious to the potentially life-threatening danger in our midst, grabbed at the chance of a lifetime and tried to scale the hurdles, scrambling up the thickly packed greenery to reach the top before tobogganing on their stomachs down the far side. Guided skilfully and calmly by the police, we were herded in the direction of a small exit, which funnelled out onto a side road. A heaving cluster of humanity bottlenecked at the gate, jostling and pushing, terrified that Armageddon was on the brink, but, for whatever reason, no one panicked. Nevertheless, Jimmy and I were both terrified, and the thought of being squashed in a confined space among such a spillage of our fellow men, many of whom were far from sober, and with no means of escape, was a horrendous prospect, let alone the threat of being bombed into oblivion.

Help came when a man in official uniform recognised Jimmy and indicated for us to follow him, leading us to a Portakabin belonging to the catering unit - far enough, he assured us, from where the alleged device was planted. The hut was as cold as a morgue and rivulets of condensation, caused by the closely packed human bodies and breath, ran down the windowpanes. The room was spartanly furnished with only a few plastic chairs (all occupied), so we sat on the floor. A continuous stream of people entered the temporary haven, hauling in their wake heavy-duty bin liners, which they emptied straight onto the floor, revealing their contents to be mountains of cash. Deftly separating the paper money from the metal, they explained that, as soon as the alarms went off in the restaurant, before running for safety, the bar staff knew the drill to empty the tills' contents into black bags. The atmosphere was surreal.

No one had a clue if a bomb was going to go off and, if it did, whether we would be blown to smithereens. I don't know how long we remained in there, but finally the all-clear was given and we were allowed to evacuate the ground. The crowd in the lane had thinned to a trickle and we walked hastily towards the main gate in the hope that I could fetch my bag from the BBC box. Since there was to be no further racing that day, we could then leave for Sussex.

An elderly couple emerged from their bungalow and, taking pity on us, invited us in for a cup of tea. We were, by that time, chilled to the bone and the thought of being in warm, safe surroundings was more than welcome. We weren't the only refugees, and they told us that they understood no one was allowed to retrieve their cars, probably not until the next day, as sniffer dogs were still patrolling the area. Realising we were going nowhere and needed somewhere to spend the night – and remember that this was the pre-mobile phone era – Jimmy asked if he could ring the BBC in London. Poor Karen (Jimmy's secretary) had been inundated with phone calls from stranded members of the outside broadcast sports team, but she pulled out all the stops and managed to secure us two maids' bedrooms under the rafters of the Atlantic Hotel in Liverpool.

When we finally got there the foyer was a swirling kaleidoscope of lovat green, subtle earthy tweeds, brown felt trilbys and the glinting of binocular lenses decked with garlands of colourful badges, interrupted here and there by a rainbow of jockeys' silks, as they too had been forced to abandon ship. We learned that Des, who had been close by HRH Princess Anne, followed speedily in her slipstream and both were able to get away before all gates were locked, Des by car, the Princess in her helicopter.

The next morning after breakfast we made our way back to the track in the hope of regaining our car. When we arrived a small group had already amassed at the main gate, where we spotted Charlie Brooks (now married to Rebekah Wade) who, in spite of being on crutches, a leg in plaster, was in cheery fettle. Jimmy once provided Charlie (when a pupil at Eton and contemporary of David Cameron) with tickets for the Coventry v Manchester United game on Boxing Day.

Charlie wrote 'Although Manchester didn't manage to win the

match was a master piece. I have to admit, some of the Sky Blue's [*sic*], especially from the corners were brilliant, and the last goal was amazing.'

We waited ... and waited ... and waited. Devoid of any news, after a couple of hours everyone was thoroughly fed up, the fragile atmosphere aggravated when a man apologetically threaded his way to the front of the queue only, to some people's selfish satisfaction, to be turned away. Frayed tempers evaporated when, in tears, he explained that his elderly Labrador bitch had been shut up in his car since the day before. Thankfully, when they were reunited, his dog, although thirsty and desperate to relieve herself, was none the worse for wear.

I don't know how long we stood in the cold, but when a 'Jobsworth' appeared behind the railings, a wave of expectancy rippled through the crowd. We watched with anticipation as he climbed a stepladder and, using a loud hailer, ordered us for some inexplicable reason to go to another gate a couple of hundred yards away.

The 'bomb' incident turned out to be a mammoth hoax conspired by the IRA to cause the maximum embarrassment on the greatest day in the British racing calendar. Reminded brutally of our own mortality, we thanked God we survived to tell the tale.

On 22 December 1997, Des invited us to have dinner at the Riverside Café, London to celebrate Rose's birthday. Michael Grade (now Baron Grade of Yarmouth, CBE and Charlton supporter) was sitting at an adjacent table and, old friends from the LWT days, they acknowledged each other. Michael was sporting a pair of scarlet socks. Without warning, Jimmy stood up, walked over and lifted his trousers, revealing novelty socks decorated with footballs I had given him for his birthday. Michael and his guests looked even more bemused when he pressed a hidden button on his ankle, causing the theme tune from *Match of the Day* to strike up. To quote Steve Coogan's alter ego Alan Partridge, it was a classic case of 'back of the net!'

A fan of the double Windsor knot, Jimmy never wore a pre-made bow tie. Before an evening out, when a dinner jacket was in order, we made a selection from his assortment of club ties, plain black ones in satin, silk and velvet or festive ones in green and red – generally reserved for Christmas gatherings. One day England were due to play a match – goodness knows against whom – and I thought (with my editorial hat on) it would be amusing if, on the programme, Jimmy wore a white tie emblazoned with the patriotic cross of St George. I went to Brighton, but the shop had run out of plain white ones. Rather than abandon the idea, I bought a white silk bow tie and asked Jimmy to put it on so that I could position marks for the red lines. The bow tie became a regular feature each time England played.

France was the host country for the World Cup in 1998 and the BBC was based in Paris. When Scotland were due to play I bought a ready-made blue bow tie and stitched a cross of St Andrew in white ribbon. My problem was how to get it to France in time for the match. Christine, my then sister-in-law (who worked at Gatwick Airport), put the bow tie on a plane with a courier, and it arrived at the BBC's bird's-nest studio on top of the Arc de Triomphe with minutes to spare before the kick-off.

Before Romania were due to play Tunisia in Marseille on 26 June the entire Romanian team dyed their hair canary yellow. When the BBC panel theorised the reason behind this madcap action in terms of whether or not it was legal, Jimmy stood out from the crowd, suggesting that they had done it purely to gain an advantage over their opponents. No one took him seriously. Relentless he persisted; however small the advantage, it is still an advantage, and with their vivid yellow hair (in addition to their matching red strip), peripheral vision would help in making a split-second decision. Whatever the truth of the matter, they drew 1–1.

After the final (the host nation beat Brazil 3–0) in July, Jimmy was free to take his annual holiday. We drove over to France expecting BBC's Head of Sport to get in touch. Des Lynam wrote in his auto-biography *I Should Have Been at Work*:

Jimmy was experiencing his last big event for the BBC. He had shaken hands a couple of years before on a two-year agreement that would take him up to and including this World Cup but his contract would not be extended beyond. Jimmy would be seventy years of age during the tournament, but he was less than pleased that the end of his BBC career was in sight. He felt he had plenty left to offer. Before our last programme it was suggested to me that, on behalf of everyone, I should wish Jimmy good luck in his retirement. Knowing him well, I realised that I had better mention the plan to him. 'Don't do that,' he said. 'I'm not retiring. The BBC have chosen not to renew my contract, that's all. I still want to work.' And so Jimmy's last hurrah was uncelebrated on our last show together.

As Des stated so clearly, despite the fact that he had fronted *Match of the Day* for 25 years, there was no farewell tipple for Jimmy. The closing of the BBC door was abrupt and, to quote from T. S. Eliot's poem 'The Hollow Men', 'Not with a bang but a whimper'.

The status quo was restored when the channel made a pleasing documentary entitled *Are You Watching Jimmy Hill?* Will Wyatt, Chief Executive of the Corporation, wrote:

I hope that you enjoyed the programme about you as much as I did. I thought that it was warm and entertaining and it paid proper tribute to your achievements in football over the years. Older viewers, such as myself, were reminded of these achievements; younger viewers may well have learned about them for the first time. Anyway, I do hope that you felt that it did justice to your contribution to the game and that it signalled an affectionate *au revoir* from the BBC. Thanks for all you have done.

37

The Sky's the Limit

With time on our hands we decided to have some work done to the house and Jimmy promised me my first grown-up, bespoke kitchen. A week after the demolition work on the old units began Sky Television got in touch, and Vic Wakeling (the channel's Head of Sport) came down to Sussex. The house was in chaos: I had no work surfaces, and a single cold tap dangling on a pipe – but no sink – which meant I had to wash up in the downstairs cloakroom. But lunch proved an unmitigated success and Sky asked Jimmy to front his own programme, *The Last Word*, comprising one-on-one interviews with big names in sport, mainly football. On 2 September Sky Sports News announced its latest signing:

Press Release – Sky Sports News – 2 September 1998.
Jimmy Hill is possibly the only person in the history of football to have been player, coach, manager, director and finally chairman of a Football League club. This experience has given him a unique insight into the game, its passions and its problems. He was a player with Brentford Football Club between 1949–52. Then he played for Fulham Football Club from 1952–61. In 1961 he led the Professional Footballers' Association in its successful struggle to lift the £20 maximum wage. Between 1961 and 1966, as manager, he took Coventry City from the Third to the First Division (now the Premier League) where they have remained ever since. In 1968 he became Head of Sport at the newly formed London Weekend Television and rose to Deputy Controller of Programmes before joining the BBC as a presenter on *Match of the Day*. From 1975 to 1982 he was unpaid managing director of Coventry City Football Club and

took over as chairman from 1980 to 1982. Since 1973 he has made over 600 appearances on *Match of the Day* and many more in other BBC sporting flagships such as *Sportsnight* and *Grandstand*. He hosted BBC radio programmes, including *Summer Sounds*, *Start the Week* and *Team Choice*, which he originated. He has made guest appearances on most of the leading chat and light entertainment shows over the years including *Wogan!*, *Parkinson*, *Blankety Blank* and *You Bet!* with Bruce Forsyth.

Mostly though, apart from soccer, he is associated with outdoor sport including hunting, golf and tennis. He retired as chairman of Fulham FC in 1997, the club for whom he played in 300 games. His distinctive face *à la* Trinder and Forsyth makes him instantly recognisable with the public, whatever their interests. In his career he has done most things including playing the trumpet and, in the past couple of years, he has taken part in several major television commercials, for example Heineken lager and Reebok.

Jimmy was awarded the OBE for services to football in 1995. Hodder & Stoughton published his autobiography *The Jimmy Hill Story*, which he wrote entirely himself, on 3 September 1998. He has just left the BBC after 25 years to join BskyB's new digital channel Sky Sports News. He has signed a four-year contract to front a programme specially created for him, *The Last Word*, which will involve personal, head-to-head interviews with high profile sportsmen not necessarily from the world of football.

We drove to the studios in Isleworth for the official photo call. Kirsty Gallacher (daughter of champion golfer Bernard) was also about to start a new career with the channel and shared the limelight that day with Jimmy. Later, during a phone interview, Jimmy was asked what he would miss most from the BBC. 'My parking space!' he replied.

During that four-year period the list of people Jimmy interviewed reads like a veritable football *Who's Who*. Preserved for eternity, these interviews are precious reminders of men who have made their mark on the game, as many have sadly passed on. The first person to face the camera was Gordon Taylor (Chairman of the PFA). I wrote in the book I kept for Jimmy's expenses, 'Clothing: navy blazer, cream shirt, blue and cream silk tie.'

Next under the spotlight was Terry Venables, followed by Kevin Keegan, George Graham, Harry Redknapp, Ruud Gullit, Johnny Haynes, Malcolm Allison, Sir Walter Winterbottom, Jimmy Greaves, Jack Charlton, Brian Clough, a young Frank Lampard, Alan Shearer, Lawrie McMenemy and countless others.

I worried every time Jimmy travelled by car to London or elsewhere at night, particularly when weather conditions were dangerous. Unable to sleep, from midnight onwards I would stand anxiously at the upstairs window waiting to catch the beam of his headlights and, as soon as they shone on the oak trees at the end of the lane, I would rush downstairs to open the gate so that he could drive straight in. This habit started when I lived in Pembridge Crescent, when Ulla and I would take up our position at the sitting-room window. Once during the FIFA World Cup in 1978, which was taking place in Argentina, and Jimmy was based at the BBC in Wood Lane, London. Daybreak was imminent and Jimmy still hadn't returned from the previous night's broadcast. I began to panic and, against my better judgement, rang Broadcasting House. The chap on duty informed me, 'No. Mr Hill hasn't left. Neither has Mr Coleman. They are busy putting the world to rights.'

Jimmy is a most sensitive, and self-deprecating man, as was Sir Edward Heath on the occasion in March 1999 when we went (along with Des and Rose) to have lunch with our ex-Prime Minister at his home Arundells, next to Salisbury Cathedral. On a chilly but bright spring day we arrived armed with a large bunch of flowers I had picked from the garden and a copy of Jimmy's autobiography. Sir Edward seemed genuinely touched by the dedication Jimmy had written and, human nature being what it is, turned to the index. He opened the book at the appropriate page and his face lit up, only to find that the entry was about Ted Heath the bandleader and, with good grace, he gave us a demonstration of his famous chuckle.

In November we were once again guests of Ron and Vee Shaw at a function in aid of those suffering from dyslexia, the Abracadabra Dinner and Orcshun [sic] at the Fishmonger's Hall in London. Jimmy, for once, was there simply to enjoy himself - or so he thought - since on this occasion the Shaws' friend and neighbour Jeffrey Archer was on the podium. Lord Archer had recently launched his campaign to become the Mayor of London, but an hour into the event our hosts were passed an urgent message saying that, due to certain circumstances, he was obliged to withdraw. 'James, you couldn't bale us out, could you?' Ron pleaded. Without hesitating a second, Jimmy ceased enjoying the hospitality and performed stupendously, receiving a standing ovation.

A few days later a letter came from the actress Susan Hampshire:

Absolutely everyone is saying how fantastic, sweet, charming, gracious, witty and brilliant you were when auctioning the paintings [an alphabet commissioned from contemporary illustrators such as Raymond Briggs, Quentin Blake and Helen Oxenbury] for the Dyslexia Institute - and I agree! You were so good and raised more than twice the amount of money they had hoped and that, I am sure, is because you were so warm and unaggressive and brought the best out of people. We can never thank you enough for stepping in at the last moment and being so fantastic. Darling Jimmy, you are a saint.

Had he been there, Jeffrey would have been presented with a commemorative gavel; it went home with us. Going, going, gone!

Part Four
A New Millennium – The Hijacking of a Brain

38

A Final Flurry

For several years, Jimmy had been contributing to the BBC World-wide's *Match of the Day* magazine entitled *Jimmy Hill's Chinwag*, interviewing such luminaries as Greg Dyke, David O'Leary, 'Deadly' Doug Ellis (favourite joke: 'Have you heard the one about the two Spanish fireman: Hose A and Hose B?'), Peter Kenyon, Bobbies Robson and Gould.

In spite of a good readership, in March 2001 BBC Worldwide called an end to publishing the magazine. Tim Glynne-Jones, the editor, thanked Jimmy in a letter dated March 2001:

> I will never forget the first time I met you on Holland Park Avenue to discuss the plans for the magazine, and we sat in a local café where everyone wanted to know your view on the forthcoming Euro '96. The enthusiasm and interest you showed that day never dwindled in five years, through posing for our summer advent calendar (remember Barbara??), and getting gruffly knocked by Ken Bates.

Speaking of Chelsea, Matthew Harding, invested £26.5 million in the London club, joined the board and became Vice Chairman. Tragedy struck in October 1996 on the way back from a match at Bolton Wanderers when the helicopter in which he was travelling crashed and he died along with the pilot and three other passengers.

Jimmy went to his funeral and read out this eulogy, which he had written for the occasion:

> Matthew Harding was unique,
> A laugh, a joke, a fit of pique

Only when his team was down
Did Matthew wear a mournful frown.
Otherwise his love of fun
Made life a joy for everyone.
The Bridge will not be quite the same,
Although a stand will bear his name.
Though up in heaven he'll hear the roar
Each time the Blues combine to score.
A game, a deal, a drink, a laugh,
Shall surely be his epitaph.

For many years Jimmy was a consultant for London Clubs and in January 2000 had been successful in persuading Brighton magistrates to grant a licence for a new casino in the city, in the marina. Another was planned for Southend, an application which led to considerable local opposition. The following May, Jimmy was asked once again to act on their behalf. Objection was so strong that George Carman QC, described by Neil Hamilton as being 'the most fearsome advocate in the land', was brought in. Jimmy was magnificent and pulled out all the stops, forcing Mr Carman to eat his words. Southend got its casino and, shortly afterwards, Mr Carman retired. Whether there was any possible link between these two events or whether it was coincidental, it makes a good story.

On 29 April a unique event was due to take place on Parker's Piece in Cambridge. This 25-acre area of common land in the centre of the city is said to be the birthplace of the modern game of association football, as it was there that the rules were formalised in 1863. In order to commemorate this moment in history, 'The Town' was to play 'The Gown', recreating the first official football match on Parker's Piece 137 years before, followed by the unveiling of a plaque. The Zion Eagles ('The Town') comprised a local group representing the shelters and hostels for the homeless in the area and, as its name implies, 'The Gown' was Cambridge University's First XI.

David Elleray, who had previously been a geography teacher and housemaster at Harrow School, officiated as referee, dressing in period costume of top hat, cravat and tails, while Jimmy carried out the commentary.

Before the whistle blew, Jimmy read this ode to football that he had written specially for the occasion:

Verily, it is the game of the universe, blessing players and spectators in different ways. On the field it inspires courage, both mental and physical, a fundamental quality for the ambitious in tackling (now without hacking ...), heading and guarding a goal with one's life. Speed of thought and foot are most rewarding allies. Absolute control of the ball and one's temper are admirable twin pillars of satisfaction. Mental and physical togetherness embraced in intricate, passing manoeuvres. Magical dribbling skills and thunderous shooting. Perhaps best of all is the deep satisfaction felt by the players at the final whistle of a game played artistically, with determination and skill in the true spirit envisaged by our forefathers many years ago. Collectively, on behalf of the whole world, we thank them for their vision, foresight and inestimable legacy.

In June 2000 we were invited to a party at Kensington Palace given by Prince and Princess Michael of Kent to celebrate Prince Michael's 60th birthday, their son Lord Frederick's 21st and their daughter Lady Gabriella's 18th. When his mother asked whom he would like to invite as a special guest, Freddie replied, 'Jimmy Hill.'

Once again we had to wear fancy dress (eighteenth-century *fête champêtre*) and, as we wandered through the beautiful gardens, everyone we bumped into (including our hosts) had the name of either a county or a town in England, ranging from Suffolk and Berkshire (the Earl of), Somerset (Lord Johnson, youngest son of the Duke of Beaufort) and Marlborough (the Duke of). The latter, delighted to see Jimmy, slapped him on the back and said, 'Miss you on the hunting field, old chap!'

Lord Frederick's fondness for Jimmy has not dwindled, as just before Christmas in 2013 he arranged for a huge bouquet to be delivered to our house. A letter addressed to me accompanied the flowers:

You probably won't remember me, but you and Jimmy came to my 21st birthday party back in 2000 after he and my mother

Princess Michael became friendly through their involvement with the SPARKS charity. I now live in the United States and was very sorry to read recently of Jimmy's illness. He was far and away the most insightful pundit on the BBC, bringing such a wealth of experience to the studio; the current crop is not in the same league. I have always been such a fan of his and I hoped perhaps these flowers might brighten his room. I hope you are comforted that he is at least in the perfect place with the best care. His legions of fans will always remember him as he was – and the players who know what he did for them should always be grateful.

In 2003 Jimmy's second programme for Sky, *Jimmy Hill's Sunday Supplement*, was in full spate, and although it was allegedly relayed from our kitchen in Sussex, I hate to ruin the illusion – but it wasn't.

On 29 March 2006 Heather Mills McCartney hosted a charity day for Adopt-a-Minefield at Sunningdale Golf Club and she and Jimmy got on like a house on fire. Jealous? *Moi?* Her marriage to Sir Paul under considerable stress, before giving Jimmy a copy of her auto-biography *A Single Step* (published in 2002), she wrote inside the cover: 'Bryony, you were lucky you got him first. Fancy swapping?' Now, there's a thought. At the Christmas ball in December while Jimmy was lighting up the dance floor I sat next to Princess Michael who, to my great pleasure, asked me to join the royal party's visit to Chelsea Flower Show the following May. Ma was suffering from chronic obstructive pulmonary disease and moved in with us, but she felt up to preparing supper for her and Jimmy in my absence. I caught the train to London and arrived by taxi at Kensington Palace a little early. As I was paying the driver Princess Michael appeared at a first-floor window of their apartment and, on spotting me, waved hello, saying, 'I'll be down in a minute!'

A member of staff showed me to a pretty pavilion in the garden and handed me a glass of champagne and, true to her word, minutes later HRH arrived with her husband, clutching a copy of my latest book. Our new chickens had recently begun laying and I had brought with me a box of half a dozen fresh eggs. I knew that the Princess would appreciate them because I had given her some once before at the SPARKS Christmas ball, when she told me that because her husband was away she was going to eat them all herself.

Our small party travelled the short distance to the Royal Hospital in a minibus, where we were greeted by a long line of the great and the good to whom we were presented individually. I was in my element, as not only did we have an exclusive, close-up view of the wonderful gardens but also I was able to speak to some of my horticultural heroes.

After the tour we retired to a private building for a champagne reception. The Royal Hospital had recently opened its doors to women veterans, and while I was chatting with the governor and his wife, Princess Michael came over, took me by the hand and said, 'Put your glass down. I'm going to introduce you to the Queen.' The Princess embraced her husband's cousin. 'Ma'am, may I introduce you to Bryony Hill. Bryony's written this wonderful book on gardening!' she said by way of explanation.

Having had to curtsey at school for five years to any member of staff we passed in the corridor, I managed to execute the genuflection without mishap. The Queen was dressed in pastel pink and her perfect complexion glowed in the evening light. She was exquisite. The whole occasion was a wonderful, unique experience and, blinded by Her Majesty's radiant smile, I can't recall a single word of what was said.

39

Billets Doux

If you have never met Jimmy and only know him through television you may be surprised to learn that he is an incurable romantic and a real old softie. Although not the greatest buyer of flowers (more often forecourt than forethought), for my birthday the year before I hit fifty he bought me a camellia plant and had written on the label the words, 'To my' in front of the name of the variety, *Sweetheart*. He could so easily have purchased another specimen perhaps more appropriately called *Forty Niner* – 'rich red in colour, peony-formed and very large'. When Jimmy began to spend more time in Pembridge Crescent he started to leave me cryptic messages demonstrating, which he tucked away for me to find, his love and affection. I have kept them all – there are hundreds – and when times are tough, particularly now that he can no longer express himself, I find comfort in the words.

After he had a nasty bout of flu he wrote: 'Darling, thank you for being the most loving, efficient and beautiful nurse in the world! It was a pleasure being unwell but better now it's over, thanks to you. 'Til Friday lunchtime, all my love and kisses, Jim the Slim.'

After I had been ill he left another: 'Many happy returns to the flat. May you be healthier, wealthier and wiser apart from lovelier, thinner and hungrier. I send impatient love, kisses and cuddles to my darling, dearest patient.'

This one was written before he left for the Cheltenham races: 'Darling love, I've got into a rush again, but promise to rush back, too! All my love, Jim the Punter,' followed soon after by this when I had been on yet another diet: 'To bony B, do put some stones in your pockets in case it becomes windy and you may blow in the wrong direction! Back soon, my angel, Overweight 'Orace.'

When I was still living in Westcroft Square my landlady Bridget's niece Stephanie Knapp lived next door. Stephanie's father Stefan, a Polish artist and sculptor who worked in enamel paint, after having been held prisoner in a gulag during the Second World War, came to England, where he joined the RAF and flew Spitfires. When we bought our house in France we became friendly with Nick Ryman, who owned the most romantic of châteaux (haunted to boot) with an award-winning vineyard in the Bergeracois hills near Monbazillac. At the entrance to his estate was an enamel panel – created by Stefan. How strange life is.

Stephanie invited me to supper and one of the guests was Erin Pizzey, who came to public knowledge for having opened a refuge (the first of its kind) in Chiswick for women and children at the mercy of domestic violence. The meal included a very garlicky salad. Jimmy joined the party after broadcasting *Match of the Day* and stayed for a glass of wine, after which we left for home. The next day I found a note stating: 'Miss POO', written in kisses.

Here are a few more precious messages:

- 'Eric [Grove] and Tom [Wilson] have made me late, not too late to say you're lovely!'
- 'Bxxxxy, Southwold Sam awaits the pleasure of your company! Love, love, love, J, J, J, xxx'
- 'B, it's wonderful to be back – even asleep. My next trick is to turn Dozy Dai into Wide-awake Walter. 'Til tea for two time. You're lovely!'
- 'Saturday Sam, alias Friday Fred, alias Thursday Theo, has become Monday Mick. XXXX J XXXX'
- 'To my most beautiful Valentine: you think of so many things to make me happy and I do notice, sweet, kind girl. I feel very inadequate sometimes but I'll be back to happiness soon and back with all my love and kisses on Wednesday.'
- '1982 – New Year Resolutions: J – 13st 7lb – 12st 10lb. B – 9st 7lb – 8st – 10lb [I wish]. Darling, thank you for last year. It was wonderful despite all the problems. You'll understand if I want to see less of you this year, and I'll try to

make sure you see less of me! Love, love and love, Sydney the Sylph.'

- 'All my love and kisses to the girl whom Jimbo misses. Here's to the time I see my wonderful Miss B.'
- 'B - you're smashing and I'm getting very fond of you! Love, love and love, XXX'
- 'To my darling wife, more beautiful than the flowers she grows and more scrumptious than the vegetables!'
- 'I've a dog whom I love
But if push came to shove,
I've a wife whom I love even more.
It's her birthday today
And if thought came to stay
I just couldn't love her much more.'

40

Labrador Rescue

When people ask me if I have had children my reply is, 'No. I've only had Labradors and they've all had ASBOs, so it's probably just as well.' Eventually I accepted the fact that I would never be the earth mother I had dreamed of being since a little girl and poured my love into looking after our yellow Labrador, and Jimmy. I shall never forget the day George had to be put to sleep. For a couple of weeks I could see that he was struggling, and although we had been able to control hip problems, at the age of nearly 14 we were on borrowed time. Then he stopped eating and started barking through the night. It was time to let go.

Jimmy had to drive to London for a meeting; I rang our vet, who said he wanted his chief nurse with him but couldn't get to the house until noon, which meant waiting for over three hours. When the team arrived George was on his favourite sofa, sleeping peacefully, and by 12.30 it was all over.

The pain in my heart was unbearable and, on writing these words, it hurts just as much as it did then. Jimmy didn't want another dog because of the tie. After a gap of three years with no replacement dog, one afternoon Hugh and Lindsay Campbell dropped by for tea. Hugh, like Jimmy, was a member of the Berkshire Golf Club, where they played frequently together, Hugh accompanied by Callie and Jimmy, of course, by George. Hugh could see no reason why we couldn't take on another four-footed friend because, if we went away, we could have house sitters. Problem solved.

In March 2001 Ipswich were home to Coventry and we went to stay in Suffolk with the Pearmans. Jimmy and I rarely spent weekends away, and this was a treat. The same could be said of Mark, whose professional demands at Sky gave him little opportunity of leading a normal life, and any time spent with his young daughters was precious. Over breakfast Mark mentioned that there was a litter of nine Labrador puppies at the farm next door and, if we wanted, we could go and see them. I could see Jimmy was reluctant and so could Mark. 'Don't worry;' he assured us, 'they are all spoken for. In fact the proposed owners are coming down this afternoon to view the puppies they have reserved.' I wanted to stay behind, but the draw was too strong. As I approached the farm gate I saw Jimmy coming down the path, a tiny, fudge-coloured bundle tucked inside his coat.

'Isn't he adorable?' he said, kissing the puppy's head.

'Don't do this to me,' I pleaded, 'you know we can't have him.'

Liz, the breeder, came up to us carrying two more from the litter. 'I couldn't help but hear what Jimmy has just said, but there is a possibility that there might be one left, either Shorty [the one Jimmy was cuddling] or one of the other boys. I'll know by five this afternoon.'

Mark and Jimmy went off to the football and we girls went into Sudbury. Everywhere we looked there were Labradors, both real and stuffed, noses snuffling under gates, piled in the back of Land Rovers and featuring on greetings cards, as though the breed was going out of fashion. We arrived back at the house at 5.15 p.m. and Mark's two daughters rushed to the telephone, whose red light was flashing. I crossed my fingers and prayed for all I was worth. Kennedy, the youngest, pushed the rewind button: the Harley Street dentist had wanted a matching pair and, if we still wanted him, Shorty was ours.

Charlie, as we re-named him, should have remained with his mother for another ten days but, because he was different from the rest with his tiny legs, his siblings bullied him and Liz thought it wise for us to take him home with us that weekend in order to spare him further distress. The next day we took him to see our vet Roger Green, who happened to be President of the Royal College of Veterinary Surgeons that year, and whom I have known all my life, to have the little man checked over. We discussed our fears of dwarfism and what the future might hold. While Roger gently manipulated

Charlie's hips he fell asleep and Roger said, 'Well, you have a perfect little specimen, albeit with a few design faults.'

Terrified of his own shadow and with a multitude of other complex problems, including an allergy to every single indigenous tree, grass and plant in the British Isles (which at one point resulted in him losing all the fur on his head and tummy), no dog could have been loved more. He was unique. A one-off. On the plus side, everything on our coffee table was safe from his permanently wagging tail! Charlie became a star both locally and nationally and lived until he was 11 years old, a miracle in itself. In the end it was cancer and not the achondroplasia (the form of dwarfism with which he was afflicted) which put an end to such a complicated life, and if ever an animal can bring happiness, it was our darling boy. Altogether, clap hands, here comes Charlie. RIP.

41

Al Bowlly, Al Jolson, Al Capone, Alzheimer's et al.

Alzheimer's: Progressive mental deterioration that can occur in middle or old age, due to generalized degeneration of the brain. It is the commonest cause of premature senility. Origin: early 20th century: named after Alois Alzheimer (1864-1915), the German neurologist who first identified it.
—Oxford English Dictionary

In his book *A Summer of a Dormouse*, John Mortimer writes tenderly about his friend the painter John Piper who had 'entered the Alzheimer world years before he died and closed the door after him'. Just like Jimmy, the artist became increasingly confused, for example substituting his fork for a pen. The Pipers had a son, Edward, another talented painter, who died unexpectedly from cancer, and John's wife Myfanwy was left to grieve on her own as her husband was beyond understanding what had happened. A similar situation in July 2009 occurred when Bobby Robson died, also from cancer, and I had the tough decision whether or not to tell Jimmy for fear of upsetting him, even though it would be forgotten in moments.

My cousin Chris Shaw, Professor of Neurology and Neurogenetics at King's College London, at the cutting edge of research into neurodegenerative disorders has given the following clinical description of Alzheimer's:

Nerve cells in Alzheimer's degenerate due to the accumulation of two toxic proteins: (i) amyloid, which accumulates in large spherical plaques outside nerves and damages its connections to other nerves (synapses), and (ii) tau, which accumulates in tangles inside neurons, effectively strangling their internal transport system. The damage causes a drop in a vital brain chemical, acetylcholine, that mediates cross talk between neurons and allows us to access our memories. For the most part we die with the neurons we were born with as nerve cells are rarely replaced. The clearing of potentially harmful proteins is crucial to keep neurons healthy into old age but it is these very housekeeping functions that decline with age and lead to toxic protein accumulation.

March 2007 saw the publication of my second book *A Compost Kind of Girl* (Book Guild Publishing, title thought up by Des Lynam) and we were asked to appear on UKTV's *Good Food Live*. Jolly Jeni Barnett was in the driving seat and Jimmy and I joined in with the cooking demonstrations given by chefs Liverpudlian Simon Rimmer and Brian Turner from Yorkshire. The atmosphere was relaxed and fun, and when it came to our actual interview, Jeni held the book up to face the camera, the reason for us being there. I butted in, saying there was a story behind the full-frontal watercolour of me on the jacket, which I had painted (along with all the other illustrations).

'When I had finished the picture,' I continued, 'I showed it to my brother who remarked that I hadn't made my t**s big enough, so I added another layer of paint.' Oh dear, oh deary me. In my eagerness I made two blunders, which probably put paid to any future career in broadcasting: (1) I uttered that four-letter word not realising that it is *non grata* in polite society, least of all on live television; and (2) I omitted the asterisks.

There followed a split-second hiatus. Jeni, ultimate pro that she is, broke the silence. 'Well, Bryony Hill from West Sussex, we *are* family show you know!'

Ma's health was deteriorating, and she was becoming increasingly dependent on me. Added to which I had Power of Attorney for my 96-year-old cousin Mary, who lived 45 minutes away in Crowborough in East Sussex and I had to engage carers, do her banking and take charge of any other problems which arose. Then my godmother, who lived in our village, needed help, but all I could do in the circumstances was prepare and freeze a variety of meals for her.

I have no idea how I managed to get through a day, let alone a week, with the huge commitments under which I felt I was drowning.

I was barely getting more than three or four hours' sleep on a good night and these were interrupted by horrendous nightmares, and more than once I woke myself screaming, they were so terrifyingly realistic. Rudderless and spinning uncontrollably into a maelstrom, I was heading full pelt for meltdown.

Jimmy continued to keep a full diary of engagements, and Sky's loyalty and kindness was limitless, an example of which was when he was taken ill during a SPARKS golf tournament at Burwood Lakes in Berkshire. He told me later (typical him!) that he was peeved at having to bale out as his team were doing extremely well and were in the frame for First Prize.

I rang the hospital and spoke to the surgeon, who told me they were keeping Jimmy under observation, and there was little point in me going there that evening. Another problem presented itself: how to collect his car from Burwood Lakes?

My main concern was what to do about Sky. If Jimmy had to undergo surgery then there was no way he would be in a fit state to broadcast live on Sunday. In desperation I rang Vic Wakeling, whose immediate reaction was for me to stop worrying about the programme and get Jimmy well again. Without hesitation he arranged for his driver to be at my disposal for as long as I needed and the next day he picked me up and took me to Reading. All was well in the end and Jimmy performed impeccably on Sunday.

In June, at her request, Ma moved back to her own home with a live-in carer which allowed her to see all her old friends in familiar surroundings. Ten days later she caught a chest infection and, on 7 July 2007, she passed away. Before she died she stipulated two things: Morris dancers at her humanist funeral, and her ashes to be scattered in Sainsbury's car park referring to the supermarket as her 'Country Club', since she knew so many people there. Unfortunately the local Morris dancing group were all busy with their day jobs, and when I told the registrar what I planned to do with the ashes she was shocked.

'Of course, you're going to disperse them when it's closed, aren't you?'

'Absolutely not,' I replied, 'she talked about it for years and if that's what she wanted, that's what we'll do.'

I chose a gloriously sunny, hot Saturday afternoon, decanted Ma into a plastic bottle carrier (what better?) and set off for Haywards Heath. The place was heaving with shoppers busily preparing for a barbecue fest and, as fate would have it, her favourite parking bay by the trolleys was free, a buddleia growing in a bed nearby.

At the end of July Jimmy retired from Sky, hanging up his microphone for good, and two months later, on 12 September (on what would have been Ma's 85th birthday), our bubble was burst when he was officially diagnosed with early onset Alzheimer's.

Carole (Watcham) has been part of the family for over eight years, having previously worked in residential nursing homes – an experience that proved invaluable. When Jimmy's needs increased (I was constantly being urged to get some sort of help) she offered to come over on Wednesday afternoons to spend it with him and then stay with us overnight, sleeping along the passage from his bedroom. Carole's dedication has been my salvation and I will never be able to thank her for all she has done, much of which was way beyond the call of duty.

Not long after Carole came to our aid I read a review of a book written by psychiatrist Oliver James called *Contented Dementia*, based on the SPECAL method (Specialised Early Care for Alzheimer's), and I ordered a copy. There was no mumbo-jumbo, no American psychobabble, but instead basic, straightforward common sense: 1) don't ask questions, 2) don't contradict and, 3) go with the flow. The sensible words and advice provided me with the lifeline I so desperately needed and, if I followed these three simple rules, day-to-day existence became bearable.

I contacted Penny Garner, who launched the SPECAL method of managing dementia, in order to make sure that I hadn't committed any blunders in my interpretation of the guidelines given in Oliver's book.

We kept in touch (one of our telephone conversations lasted over two hours ...) and in this email, she says:

As I mentioned during our fascinating conversations, there is such an upbeat note to your own description of reading/

practising what is in Oliver's book. At the same time there have been moments of paradox for me when I simultaneously resonate with your powerful and compellingly authentic words, yet find I am passionately motivated to signpost that well-being in dementia really is possible not just at the start but all the way through to the very end of the care journey. I feel it is so important that families know about this extraordinary possibility.

Having lived through caring for a loved one with Alzheimer's and with the information I have gleaned from *Contented Dementia*, I have put together a sort of *aide mémoire* of important 'rules' (in the hope that it might help others in a similar situation) in order to maintain 24-hour wraparound care and love. Of course, no two people are the same but, with dementia, there is a definite (albeit random) course along which the relentless stream of this awful illness flows. To continue with the analogy, there will be shallow parts where the water is calm and tranquil, only to be disrupted when boulders and rocks appear, creating waves. There will be crashing waterfalls too, but when the banks widen as the river approaches the sea, the ebb and flow will cease and the end of the journey is reached.

1. ***Do not ask questions – make a statement***. Someone who has Alzheimer's, by default, has little (if any) memory of the present although they may retain details of their past life. In trying to have a conversation by asking a question you are putting them on the spot, which is confusing and frightening. For example, do not ask, 'Did you enjoy your supper?' Firstly, they won't recall having eaten let alone what was on the menu. Get around it by presenting a statement, for example 'I really enjoyed that chicken/fried egg/ham etc.' This removes any pressure.

2. ***If an appointment is in the diary, do not mention it beforehand***. Say, 'Let's go in the car for a nice drive,' and leave it at that.

3. ***Never, ever contradict***. If they think they have been to India via Australia, let it be – just don't take that particular airline!

4. ***Go with the flow***. Perhaps this is the most important – and the hardest to achieve. Please don't think this is patronising. By entering into their world you are being kind. In *Contented Dementia* (sorry, Oliver – I might have got some of the facts wrong, as I lent your book to a friend!) there is the incident of a man who had been a soldier and suffered from post-traumatic stress and became agitated and frightened by sudden loud noises. One day, during lunch, a saucepan fell to the floor in the kitchen a clatter, which sent him into a blind panic. He left his chair and rushed under the table. On seeing his distress, a carer joined him and said, something along the lines of, 'Goodness! That was a large one! Let's wait a moment. Listen. We've got the all clear. We can come out now. It's perfectly safe.' The shaking stopped and he returned to his chair.

5. ***Do not bombard them with too much information***. Keep instructions simple.

6. ***Boost their confidence by complimenting them***. If they wish to help in the kitchen give them a simple task, even if it is not carried out correctly or, as you would wish. It doesn't matter. Thank them for their kindness and they will feel important and of use.

7. ***Try not to move the goalposts***. Changes in any form cause upset such as work being carried out in the home, sudden noises, or strangers are all potentially disturbing factors. Try and keep things on as even a keel as is humanly possible. Among some distracting techniques are: television, music, animals, picture books or a walk in the fresh air away from it all.

8. ***Anger and how to control it, yours as much as theirs***. With Alzheimer's mood swings are par for the course. Above all, don't react – ignore it completely and above all try not to be worried or frightened. The SPECAL method

divides moods or feelings into two categories, each with its own colour; ordinary, level calm times are 'green'. This is what life is like for most of us most of the time and what you are aiming to achieve 100% of the time.

'Red' is when the alarm bells start to ring, for example when a question is asked and there is no back-up information. This produces panic, panic, ***panic***! The best thing is to avoid anything that can trigger these 'red' feelings; by not asking questions or contradicting can make a huge difference, or taking speedy action to defuse a potential problem. 'Silly me!' works ever so well. These moments are not self-inflicted and it's our responsibility to ensure they don't happen.

If anger does come to the surface, do the following: count to three (or 30 if necessary). Walk out of the room, pause for a short moment, swear blue murder and get if off your chest then go back inside with a beaming smile, as if nothing untoward has happened and say, 'I'm going to make us a lovely cup of tea,' or 'it's tea time.' Job done.

9. ***Useful calming words which defuse a difficult situation.*** Make a list of events in their life or familiar words which bring back happy memories. It might be a favourite holiday location, a special anniversary, food, a pet, a song, anything you can think of. By choosing them at random you will soon learn which are the most effective.

10. ***Repetition.*** Perhaps this has to be the hardest to handle and which will try your patience to stretching point. Take a deep breath, calm down and reply gently – even if you have done so ten times in as many minutes. For them, it is the first time they have asked the question. You may notice that one particular answer seems to be 'right' even if it isn't correct from your point of view. If so, remember not to contradict.

11. ***Body language.*** Someone with Alzheimer's has a unique radar system and recognises changes in body language like no other. You must never show signs of irritation. However slightly you think you have gritted your teeth or shrugged

your shoulders in (quite natural) exasperation, they will notice - it might just as well have been posted up on 20-foot high billboards and the chances are they will become angry. You have to have the patience of a saint, and believe me, although this is hard to accomplish you can achieve it over time with practice. The good side of this is that, if you show warmth, happiness, pleasure they will notice and share it.

12. ***One final point.*** However hard it is to be with someone with Alzheimer's, please don't give up on them. Continue to communicate, to keep in touch. They may have reached the point where they no longer recognise familiar friends and faces but they respond to a hug and a hand held. Look them in the eye and smile. If we all do our share, this last stage of life will remain full of happy instant moments, devoid of anxiety and full of peace, warmth and above all the feeling that they are special. Tell them (even if it breaks the habit of a lifetime) you love them.

42

A Downward Spiral

'It's so sad that someone as vital and dynamic as your Jimmy is now in nursing care. I hope that he's as happy as the last time we met at the lovely party in your home. Jimmy Hill was a fine sportsman, a great footballer and intensely competitive. I played pro-celebrity golf with him and was glad he was on my side! A true Corinthian, a gentleman. Was there ever a man of better humour, of better heart?' Sir Terry Wogan confided to me.

There is no way to sugar-coat Alzheimer's. It is an illness which is ruthless in its lack of discrimination; young, old, intelligent, everyone could be a target. I started writing a diary to use as a dumping ground – an emotional dustbin – for all the frustration and anger caused by the terrible upheaval in our lives.

I was constantly told, 'But he looks amazing! I had a great conversation with him in the High Street. Frankly, you would never know there was anything wrong.' Their assumption that I was exaggerating matters or, worse, making it up, hurt. I accepted that their (quite natural) lack of understanding was, for want of a better word, understandable. Unless you have had personal dealings with someone with Alzheimer's you can have no idea what it entails. There is no escape, no safety net, nothing except the certainty that this is as good as it gets.

I cannot tell you how hard it is to watch someone you love disappear in front of your eyes. I have been a poor sleeper for many years, permanently on the *qui vive*, and I keep a notepad by the bed because inspiration often hits me in the wee small hours and if I don't write the ideas down they will have evaporated by morning. I happened to have purchased a copy of Jennifer Saunders' book in a charity shop. One night, at 3.35 a.m., I was bursting with thoughts but I discovered I had left my pad in the kitchen. Rather than go downstairs and risk waking Suzie (my new Labrador), I grabbed the first thing to hand: Jennifer's book, as yet unread. I opened it on the almost blank title page and scribbled like mad. About to turn off the light, I noticed that Mrs Edmondson's tome is entitled *Bonkers* which summed me up perfectly and I laughed out loud at the irony.

Alzheimer's affects everyone differently and there are specific stages of the disease when parts of the brain shut down randomly, never to be retrieved. Some sufferers, gentle beings in their previous life, may become foul-mouthed and aggressive monsters, and others of a more rumbustious nature, meeker individuals. I likened it to a large office block where a light bulb blows on the ninth floor but no one goes to replace it. Then, maybe a week or so later, two bulbs go on the ground floor and again, no new ones are fitted. Next, one conks out in a cupboard. This continues until there are few – if any – light bulbs left in working order and, in time, the building lies empty until it crumbles to the ground. In the real world we would sack the managing agents, but with Alzheimer's the contract is open-ended.

In the Fifties, when Jimmy was playing professionally, synthetic substances such as vinyl were not used in the construction of the ball. Instead cowhide which, being of natural origin and thus varying in thickness, was cut into panels, stitched together and lined with an inflatable rubber bladder. Before a home match, Jimmy said that they used to immerse the ball in a bucket of water overnight and, the leather being porous, it gained considerably in weight by the time the whistle blew for the kick-off. The visitors would be expecting to play with a normal ball, so after a soaking (although it would have affected both teams equally) the home team would have the edge over their rivals. Can it therefore be purely coincidental that so many ex-professional footballers have developed dementia? Was it caused by the constant heading of these heavy balls? Research is currently being undertaken to see if persistent pounding contact with a foreign body, be it the ball or another player, could be damaging to the brain. Recently FIFA made a ruling that if a player is concussed or suffers a head injury it is the doctor who makes the decision as to whether he should be taken off the field in order to be fully assessed,

205

only allowing him to return to the game when deemed fit. This could be for any length of time from hours to a week depending on the seriousness of the injury. In the good old days it was up to the coach to make this judgement when, more often than not, the player was treated with the magic sponge, patched up and sent back on the pitch.

43

Support for Me – That's What Friends Are For

Friendship is the hardest thing in the world to explain. It's not something you learn in school. But if you haven't learned the meaning of friendship, you really haven't learned anything.

—Muhammad Ali

It is now over three years since my darling man had to go into care and I am adjusting to the fact that he will never come home. I have accepted that this was the only solution, and with the passing months the feeling of having failed him is finally beginning to assuage, but this partial release from responsibility is a double-edged sword and has brought about its own deep brand of guilt. If it hadn't been for a hard core of loving, caring and loyal group of friends and family I would have crumbled.

Carole C-J said, 'Dearest Bryony, you are a tower of strength and have managed so well as carer-in-chief but now that his mind has deteriorated further you have taken a wise decision, one that is undoubtedly the best for Jimmy and for you too. It must seem strange being on your own – a peculiar mix of delight in your newly found "freedom" and sadness in no longer sharing your life and home with Jimbo. Take care of yourself, dearest friend.'

Carolyn Pretty wrote: 'I'm so sad for you and James. It must be heart wrenching watching him go through this having been so vibrant all his life. You have been a star. Don't you forget it but I know you wouldn't have it any other way. I will never forget your face in the kitchen when he danced with you.'

'You are a wonderful wife. Jimbo just doesn't know how lucky he was when your paths crossed. Jules (Higgins).'

Lawrie McMenemy told me, 'No one could have looked after Jimmy better. You are the best thing that ever happened to him and the best thing he ever did was marry you.'

Cliff Morgan sent a postcard: 'Dearest Bryony, oh Bryony – Pat and I are so sad that Jimmy is in a nursing home. Jimmy was such a great friend to so many; a wonderful gift to football, a genuine communicator for the BBC – a rich life – a generous life – he gave his all. We are so honoured to be friends of yours; as the poet wrote: "Many people walk in and out of your life but only true friends leave footprints in your heart." You are a blessing.'

Clare Oldridge (an old schoolfriend) said, 'I am sorry that Jimmy has finally gone into a care home. It cannot have been an easy decision and must have been with a very heavy heart, but I'm sure you realized that there just came a point where there was no more you could do on your own. You can only say to yourself that you did everything possible to keep him at home and happy for many more extra years than other mortals might have done. So I salute you for being so unselfish and so brave.'

Lady Winter-bottom (Walter's widow) rings every year on Jimmy's birthday. She wrote to me recently and said, 'Bryony dear, I have so many lovely memories. Jimmy is so lucky to have you for his wife.'

Finally, Tim Brooke-Taylor emailed: 'Although it's sad that Jimmy is in the position he's in, at least he is being looked after and I'm sure he is aware of your constant love. I can only remember good things about him; he has always been fun, generous and an outstanding good egg and I don't think I can say that about many people.'

44

Full Circle

The sixth age shifts into the lean and slipper'd pantaloon,
With spectacles on nose and pouch on side,
His youthful hose, well saved, a world too wide
For his shrunk shank; and his big manly voice
Turning again toward childish treble, pipes
And whistles in his sound.
Last scene of all
That ends this strange eventful history,
Is second childishness and mere oblivion.
Sans *teeth*, sans *eyes*, sans *taste*, sans *everything*.
— William Shakespeare, *As You Like It*

I read of some research into the effect of emotion on amnesia (one of the principal symptoms of Alzheimer's) carried out by Justin S. Feinstein, Melissa C. Duff and Daniel Tranel from the University of Iowa College of Medicine. This is an extract from their paper published in 2010 in *Proceedings of the National Academy of Sciences of the United States of America*:

Can the experience of an emotion persist once the memory for what induced the emotion has been forgotten? We capitalized on a rare opportunity to study this question directly using a select group of patients with severe amnesia following circumscribed bilateral damage to the hippocampus. The amnesic patients underwent a sadness induction procedure (using affectively-laden film clips) to ascertain whether their experience of sadness would persist beyond their memory for the sadness-inducing films. The experiment showed that the patients continued to experience elevated levels of sadness well beyond the point in time at which they had lost factual memory for the film clips. A second experiment using a happiness induction procedure yielded similar results, suggesting that both positive and negative emotional experiences can persist independent of explicit memory for the inducing event. These findings provide direct evidence that a feeling of emotion can endure beyond the conscious recollection for the events that initially triggered the emotion.

I visit Jimmy every two or three days if possible, not because I have to but because I want to. I cling to the hope that, if I make him smile, I have made him happy however fleeting the moment.

I received a letter from someone signing herself 'Angela', who heard my interview in November 2014 with Danny Pike on BBC Radio Sussex:

> I thought your description of the 'lights going out' is so appropriate with this awful condition. My husband was diagnosed with vascular dementia in 2008 [a year after Jimmy's Alzheimer's was confirmed] but unlike your husband he does recognise me but is unable to converse. However, like Jimmy he responds to a hug and a kiss which leaves me with the feeling that he is still well aware of my place in his life, which is what we all crave. Thank you for the comfort you gave me.

My cousin Chris gave me the following current situation regarding his research:

> A great deal of progress is being made as to why some people develop Alzheimer's and others don't. The strongest evidence is that certain gene variants predispose some people to protein accumulation. Indeed, some rare gene mutations cause an early-onset and more aggressive form of dementia that can be passed down through the generations. Head injury, diabetes and obesity all increase the risk of Alzheimer's, and there is good evidence that a healthy Japanese or Mediterranean diet, mental stimulation and physical fitness are protective.
>
> Therapies designed to boost the levels of acetylcholine do

significantly improve memory in people with Alzheimer's, but the benefit wears off over time. Great advances have been made in understanding why these proteins accumulate. Designing therapies that can help the brain clear these toxic proteins is the focus of much current research, and exciting progress is being made. It is hoped that these discoveries made in the laboratory can be translated to really effective treatments for people with Alzheimer's and may even help the disease starting in those at greatest risk.

Epilogue: The Last Word

As I reach this final page, I am assured peace will come in time, but how I wish Jimmy was with me now to enjoy the changing colours of a late-summer sunset; to watch the clouds always coming 'from the south'; to be amazed at the number of baby fish in the pond; to pick ripe, shiny apples from the tree or to sit together in companionable silence, holding hands, in the garden he adored.

And so it goes on, our love story far from over. Jimmy has had an incredible life and mine was blessed when we met. I have few, if any, regrets. This morning, when I went for a walk with Suzie, the bright winter sun warmed my back. I looked up and saw that the brilliant blue sky was a mass of kisses formed by the criss-crossing of vapour trails created by passing aircraft on their way to heaven knows where.

What if it had been me falling by the wayside? The answer is simple: my gentleman Jim would never have let me down.

B is for beautiful

R is for ravishing

Y is for youthful

O is for those momentous obvious own

N is for natural

So Y go on!

love + adoration

Ju

xxxxx

212